SHIN[illegible]

The Way of the Gods

Introduction to the Traditional Religion of Japan

DINGO
BOOK CLUB

"Great Books Change Life"

Table of Contents

Introduction

Shinto is Japanese for 'The way of the Gods.' Shinto represents Japanese religion and cult that has its origins in prehistoric times. Referred to as the '*indigenous faith of the Japan*' - the belief occupies a significant position even in the technologically advanced modern Japanese society. Shinto has held sway over the religious, social, and political way of life in Japan for over two millennia and continues its reign over the minds of the Japanese even today.

In Japan, Shinto is also referred to as *kami-no-michi*. Believed to have started around 1000 B.C.E., Shinto still holds pride of place in Japanese society. Shintoism already existed in Japan when the Chinese introduced Buddhism to the country, back in the 6th century. Shinto was born from an existing primitive form of religion that believed in nature worship. The ancient Japanese honored and worshipped sacred spirits representing the various forms of nature including rivers, mountains, valleys, storms, celestial objects, etc.

As the communities grew and expanded, people started building shrines where they could deify and worship these spirits. These shrines became the center of their social lives. When Buddhism arrived in the 6th century, Shinto-Buddhist syncretism began and progressed slowly but surely to combine elements from both beliefs. Despite the syncretism, the concepts of purification and ancestor worship are believed to be purely Shinto which continues to this very day.

The Shinto faith fascinates and mystifies the entire world. Both the casual, short-term traveler and those who have chosen to make Japan their home are enthralled by everything that represents Shinto or the Kami Way. Shinto is more than a religion. It is a way of life for the people of Japan amalgamating rituals, ideas, methods of doing things, and attitudes. Shinto is an integral part of the country and its people.

The Kami Way in Shintoism is a personal faith in the objects of worship and a belief in noble and sacred spirits. Shinto followers believe that their emperor is a divine descendant who governs the land with the help of rituals done for the deities, or Kami. Shinto ritualism takes place in hundreds of shrines all across the country. These local rites performed at each of the community shrines mirror the emperor's ceremonies. Shinto followers believe that these divine rituals help in aligning the supernatural, human, and the natural worlds harmoniously together to achieve prosperity.

The most critical aspect of Shintoism is that religion and community life are one and the same. The best personal destiny one can have is to merge the individual destiny with that of the entire community or nation. This connection between group and individuals dates back to the ancient times when a household or 'ie' was defined as the smallest and the most important unit of Japanese society.

The 'ie' was more than just a household defined as per Western thought. New, unrelated, and additional members could be adopted into the ie, and the entire household participated in its economic growth. This was the beginning of giving importance to the group over the individual, a core element in Shintoism.

This book is intended to give a basic, yet detailed view of the Shinto world for a beginner. This book traces the path of Shinto starting from its ancient origins to its present day.

Chapter 1: Introducing Shintoism

What is Shintoism?

Shintoism deals with two crucial elements:

- Devotion to spiritual beings and higher powers who are referred to as kami and
- Devotion to the performance of rituals

Shinto does not attempt to explain the world, the purpose of creation, etc. Instead, it exhorts its followers to perform rituals diligently and in a committed manner as per the stringent rules and regulations laid down in Shinto concepts. These rituals help human beings to connect and communicate with Kami.

What is Kami?

Kami is not a just a term used to refer to God. As per Shintoism, kami is a word used to represent spiritual beings, various gods and goddesses who are concerned with the welfare of humankind. These caring spiritual beings appreciate and value humankind's interest in them. They help us achieve happiness because they want human beings to be happy and prosperous.

When human beings respect and worship the spiritual beings endowed with supernatural powers, then they reciprocate it by bestowing us with benefits in the areas of health, wealth, and other materialistic pursuits.

Kami Concepts

While kami can be loosely referred to as spirits, it means a lot more in Shintoism. Calling them merely spiritual beings is inadequate although a good place to begin understanding the term. Kami, as said earlier, are very bonded to human beings, and they respond to prayers and worship. Kami have the power to influence and change human events as well as natural forces. People believe there are over eight million kami in Japan!

Many of the ideas of kami in Shintoism are interrelated, but they can rarely be interchanged. This collection of non-interchangeable ideas is not just different but also includes varied interpretations of related concepts. Kami can be used to refer to the spiritual beings, or it can be used to refer to any quality that they possess. The word kami can be applied to the core of existence that is found in everything in and around this world.

However, while kami is the core of existence, only those elements that manifest their kami-nature in an unmistakably striking way are called by this term. Kami is the mystical or sacred element in all the things in this world. It is omnipresent, omniscient, and is found everywhere. Kami is what makes every detail in this universe what it is meant to be and not something else.

Kami incorporates the following:

- A harmonizing and life-giving power called Musubi
- A truthful, honest will called Makoto

A point to note here: not all kami are good elements; some are downright evil!

By now, you must have understood that kami is complicated to explain and even harder to understand. Shinto believes that human beings have limited capabilities which make it difficult for us to understand and grasp the true nature and meaning of Kami.

Kami is represented as spiritual beings with great power to help human beings. This is the best way to start understanding the subtleties of this somewhat nebulous concept in a more tangible way. However, Kami in Shintoism is different from the gods and goddesses or, even GOD, of other religions in the following ways:

- Kami are not divine unlike the gods and goddess of other religions of the world.
- Neither are Kami omnipotent nor are they perfect; they do make mistakes and they do behave badly.
- Kami are quite similar in nature to human beings; they are only a higher manifestation of extraordinary power.
- Also, Kami live among human beings in this world. They do not live in any supernatural world or universe.

Kami include many beings and elements of this world and universe:

- They can be the gods that made and designed this universe.
- They can be the spirits residing in living beings and can also be the beings themselves.
- They can be representatives of the earthly landscapes such as lakes and mountains, as well as natural catastrophes such as earthquakes and storms.
- They can be human beings who became kami after their deaths.

To take this explanation is a bit further; kami of a mountain or river can be the mountain or river itself or the spirit that is embedded in the elements. Not all kami have been given a particular name. Some of them are simply referred to as kami of that place, thing, or person.

Types of Kami

There are many types of kami in the Shinto faith classified into different categories. Here is a method that categorizes the types of Kami based on what they manifest.

Kami of Nature

Kami are believed to reside in certain natural unique formations such as a distinctly or unusually-shaped mountain or tree, a waterfall, a large rock, a volcano, etc. the kami is manifested through the heart and faith of the worshippers when their prayers are answered. Kami of nature are manifested in other natural forces as well such as wind, rain, thunder, sunshine, fire, and more.

Kami of Deification

In this form, a dead person achieves the status of kami. Many reasons exist for giving the dead person such as status. For example, Emperor Ojin who ruled from 270 A.D. – 310 A.D. is deified as Kami Hachiman; the God of War and the country's protector. Another example is that of Sugawara no Michizane or Kami Tenman Tenjin who is now the God of Education.

Kami of Folk Worship

Also referred to as Folk Shinto, these kami are usually localized to a particular community, tribe, or clan. The kami could be a result of combining one or more of the various stories, legends, myths, superstitions, literary works, and the origin of the specific clan. Folk Shinto is very closely connected to divination and shamanism as well.

Kami of Shared Belief

They are kami that have grown from a local place and have been proselytized into national status in which all followers of Shintoism repose faith. A specific process called *bunrei* (dividing the spirit) enshrines the kami from a local place into another location. The ceremony that is conducted for this is called *kanjo*.

History of Shintoism

Shintoism, a Japanese religion and cult, is believed to have originated in the prehistoric times and continues to hold an important place in the social, political, and personal lives of the Japanese. During the early period, Shintoism did not have a name, a fixed dogma, sacred writings or texts, or moral precepts rather was only a body of religious practice and belief followed during that time. A variety of kami or spiritual beings were worshipped mostly representing the natural world such as the earth, the sky, the celestial bodies, storms, earthquakes, etc. The rituals and rites included those of thanksgiving through offerings of valuables like cloth, swords, and those of purification from defilement and crime.

Around the 6th century, this native religion was given the name Shinto to differentiate it from Confucianism and Buddhism, both of which were brought by the Chinese into Japan even though Buddhism had its roots in India. Buddhism quickly began to dominate Shinto, and Buddhist priests took over Shinto shrines and added their own artifacts, religious ornaments, and rituals into the daily rituals.

In the late 8th century and the early 9th century, Kukai - who became Kobo Daishi posthumously - a celebrated and revered Japanese teacher combined the principles of Buddhism and Shintoism and established a new religious doctrine, Ryobu Shinto, which translated to '*Shinto of two kinds.*' In this new doctrine, Buddhism and its practices and rituals dominated over those of Shintoism. Moreover, elements, ideas, and concepts were adopted from Confucianism as well.

The ancient Shinto religion that had its origins in the prehistoric era almost disappeared and was followed only at a few large and Shinto-dominated shrines and the Imperial Palace. However, the rulers and emperors themselves became Buddhists. The priests of the ancient Shinto religion became magicians and fortune-tellers.

Then, around the 18th century, notable scholars such as Hirata Atsutane, Mabuchi, and Motoori Norinaga began work to revive this forgotten 'Way of the Gods' through their teachings and writings. Highly motivated by nationalistic fervor and the reverence of all things Japanese, these men had a hatred for all things foreign including religions like Buddhism, which was not of Japanese origin.

These men began the work of disintegrating Buddhism and reviving Shintoism as the national religion of the state. In the 8th and 9th centuries, the imperial government faced threats to their sovereignty from the Ezo tribes of northern Japan. Powerful warriors called shoguns were commissioned as military commanders to lead these battles. All military commanders after this period were bestowed with the title of shogun.

Between 12th and the 19th centuries, the shoguns were the true power behind Japanese imperialism. Although, in theory, the shoguns were accountable to the emperor, in reality, the emperor was reduced to a mere symbol of sovereignty and were tightly controlled of the shoguns. The shogunate was the true empire in Japan.

From the beginning of the 18th century, the notable scholars mentioned above began the revival of Shintoism. The shogunate was overthrown, and the power of the emperor was reinstated. As per ancient Shinto beliefs, the emperor's sovereignty was a divine right bestowed on him by Amaterasu Omikami, the sun goddess who is believed to have founded the country of Japan.

From that time until 1946, Shinto had two forms; Shrine, or State Shinto, and Sectarian Shinto. The former took the form of a nationalistic patriotic cult and received ample financial support from the imperial government. However, Sectarian Shinto consisted of multiple sects formed and organized by private people based on the differences in the interpretation of the ancient form of Shinto.

During this time, shrines proliferated the entire country. The State Shinto was completely removed from the power of the imperial government when the Americans occupied Japan during World War II. The emperor also relinquished his claims to divinity, an act enforced by the Americans thanks to the power of their military at that time.

Sectarian Shinto remained unaffected and was treated on a par with the other religions of that time including Buddhism and Christianity. Today, there are five major groups of

Sectarian Shinto which are discussed in more detail under Types of Form of Shintoism later in this chapter. list which chapter

Today, a considerable percentage of the Japanese people participate in nearly all Shinto rituals, practices, and festivals. Yet, there are very few people who say that Shintoism is their sole or major religion.

Common Concepts and Stories in Shintoism Shintoism advocate many concepts, and knowledge of its terminology will help you understand the Way of the Gods better.

Kojiki – Translating to Records of Ancient Matters, Kojiki is one of the two sacred texts of Shintoism, and is the oldest existent text on this ancient religion dating back to around the 8th century A.D.

Nihon Shoki – Translating to Chronicles of Japan, this is the second sacred text of Shintoism and is far more detailed and elaborate than Kojiki. Chapter Four further details these two texts.

The Creation Story – laid out in these two texts which reveal the following concepts of Shintoism:

- Japan was the first ever land to be created in the world.
- Sexual union is a sacred process of creativity.
- Certain rituals have to be performed in order to prevent bad things from happening.

- Bad things can also happen if the natural order is disturbed.
- The woman is subordinate to the man.
- Kami and human beings are created through the same process.
- Children who are imperfect are allowed to be abandoned.

The Shinto creation story is a unique one. The universe was first created from pre-existing chaos. During the creation of the universe, multiple kami automatically appeared. The relationships between these kami brought forth a brother and a sister called Izanagi and Izanami, respectively. Izanagi translates to 'he who invites,' and Izanami translates to 'she who invites.'

The other kami gave these siblings a jeweled spear, and when they thrust it upon the ocean, the first bit of water that the spear touched became the central island of Japan. The siblings married each other and had children. Hiruko was their first-born who had a handicap and was abandoned by his parents. It is believed that the handicap was a result of Izanami speaking first during the sexual intercourse; an act that was performed and treated like a ritual.

The other children born from Izanagi and Izanami were the other islands of Japan and multiple other kami.

The Story of the Land of the Dead – While she was giving birth to the kami of fire, Izanami got burned severely and died.

Her death was considered to be the first death that occurred in the world (which is Japan for Shinto believers). Her husband, in the fury of his grief, beheaded the child, blaming it for the death of his beloved wife. More kami were born out of this execution.

Izanagi was so grief-stricken that he went to Yomi, the land of the dead, in search of his wife. But, by the time he found her, she had already consumed the fruit of the dead and was condemned to live in Yomi forever. She told him to be patient while she spoke with the rulers of Yomi to see if there is a way for her to return to the land of the living. She took a promise from her husband that he must not look at her while he waited.

But, after some time, Izanagi broke the promise he made to his wife, went in search of her, and found her. Her body was full of maggots and was in a terrible rotting state. He was terrified and wanted to go back to the land of the living. He started running away from Yomi. However, Izanami was livid at having the promise broken and was also ashamed at having been seen in that horrible state. She followed him and tried to keep him back in Yomi where he could live with her for eternity.

But, Izanagi managed to escape from Yomi. He blocked the entrance with a huge boulder to keep his wife from following him. He therefore created a permanent barrier between the land of the dead and the land of the living. Furious at the turn of events, Izanami said that she would drag 1000 people every day to Yomi. To counter it, Izanagi promised that he would create 1500 babies each day.

The following Shinto concepts are clarified here:

- Kami are not immortal beings. They can get hurt, and they can die. But they have a duty to support human beings.
- When they die, they also rot just like human bodies rot.
- Kami experience human emotions and can suffer from grief and bereavement.
- Death is not good for the community and disrupts the harmony.
- Death and decay represent the most powerful type of impurity; human beings should have nothing to do with death and should stay away from it altogether. Life is far more powerful than death.

The spirits that occupy the land of the dead are all harmful and malicious and are always looking to drag or forcibly take away human beings from the land of the living.

The story of purification and its importance in Shintoism

Even though Izanagi escaped from the land of the dead, he was still impure because of his contact with that land and its inhabitants. His contamination and impurity brought him a lot of bad luck and misfortune. He undertook the purification process by bathing and cleansing himself thoroughly in the ocean which helped him wash away the pollution of death.

This is considered to be the start of the harae purification ritual (more about that in chapter five. As Izanagi was undergoing the purification process, new kami including the Sun Goddess (Amaterasu) and the God of Wind and Storms (Susanoo) were created.

This story explains the following concepts of Shintoism:

- Kami can be polluted too, and they are not all-powerful.
- Pollution and impurity makes terrible things happen
- Impurity can be removed through purification; salt and water are potent purifying elements.
- The process of purification is very creative.

The Story of Amaterasu and Susanoo

Amaterasu was chosen by Izanagi to rule the world which angered and upset Susanoo. He behaved and threw tantrums so much so that he was exiled from heaven. Amaterasu also got angry at her brother for his misbehavior and sulked away in a cave which put the entire world in darkness. All the other kami went to the cave and tried in vain to persuade her to come out . She continued to sulk.

The other kami decided to trick her out of her cave. They had an entertainment show which had all the elements of crudity and nudity. The kami were heard laughing and having fun. Curiosity to see what was happening compelled Amaterasu to come out of her cave, at which point the other waiting kami caught and forced her to take her rightful place in the cosmos. Notably, despite being banished, Susanoo is a powerful kami worshipped at many shrines across the country for his ability to avert disasters.

The story of Amaterasu and Susanoo gives an insight into the following Shinto concepts:

- Again, kami are not omnipotent; while Amaterasu cannot be forced out of her cave-home, she can be captured when she comes out eventually.
- Kami manifest all the bad characteristics of human beings including sulking, misbehaving, laughing, and being overly curious.
- Kami love bawdy entertainment include crudity and dancing, and human beings can use this trait to please them, and get them to do things for you.

The Story of the Imperial Family

discusses the divine lineage and ancestry of Japanese emperors. Interestingly, female power is acknowledged here which is in direct contrast to the earlier stories where women allowed and expected to be subordinate to men

Amaterasu had a large family of children and grandchildren. She and other senior kami decided together that Japan would always be ruled by an Imperial family which had its origins in her family tree. She sent Ninigi, one of her grandchildren, to Japan to rule over the land. He took a sword and a mirror (the symbol of the Sun Goddess) with him.

Now, Jimmu Tenno, Ninigi's grandson is considered as the first emperor of Japan. Even today, the emperors of Japan are believed to be descendants of Ninigi, and through him, share the divinity lineage with Amaterasu. This story establishes the family of Yamamoto clan as the emperors of Japan, as they are considered the direct descendants of the Sun Goddess. The rival clan descended from Susanoo, is called the Izumo clan.

Types or Forms of Shintoism

There are many Shinto sects prevalent in Japan. Here are some of them explained in a bit of detail.

Shrine Shinto (Jinja Shinto) – is the primary and most prevalent form of Shintoism that exists today. When westerners think of Shinto, it is the Shrine Shinto sect that they visualize. This form involves a lot of worship rituals, practices, and events at the local shrines. In fact, the Association of Shinto Shrines oversees over 80,000 shrines all across the country.

Imperial Shinto (Koshitsu Shinto) – This form is exclusive to the imperial family, and the rites and rituals are performed only at the following three royal shrines, or Kyuchu Sanden, within the walls of the Imperial Palace in Tokyo:

1. *The Central Shrine or Kashiko-dokoro* – The legendary ancestress of the Imperial Family, the Sun Goddess or Amaterasu-Omikami, is enshrined here. The Sacred

Jewels, or yasakani no magatama, are also supposed to be kept in this shrine.

2. *The Ancestral Spirits Shrine or Kōrei-den* – is the place where the spirits of the dead members of the Imperial Family are enshrined one year after their deaths.
3. *The Shrine of the Kami or Shin-den* – houses deities from Shinto legends and myths

Folk Shinto (Minzoku Shinto)

Revolves around local shrines, beliefs, and the local kami of a particular tribe or community. The Folk Shinto sect is a mixture of beliefs that include spiritual healing, divination, shamanism, and even possessions by spirits. The beliefs of Folk Shinto come from Buddhism, Confucianism, and Taoism too. Folk Shinto is seen mostly in rural areas of Japan. Each community elects a local person to conduct the worship rituals and rites for the local kami of the shrine.

Sect Shinto (Kyoha Shinto)

Sect Shinto exists since the time of the Edo Period and continues to be relevant even today. The difference between Sect and Shrine forms of Shintoism is that the Sect Shintoism developed much later and more self-consciously than the Shrine Shintoism. Sect Shintoism identifies itself with a founder (a unique feature in Shintoism), a formal set of dogmas and teachings, and specific sacred writings and texts.

There are 13 different sub? Sub-sects under Sect Shinto and each of these 13 sub-sects has their own set of principles, teachings, and founding fathers. These 13 sects mostly emerged since the beginning of the 19th century. The 13 sub-sects are categorized into five major types including:

1. *Faith-healing sect* – consists of Shinto healers
2. *Pure Shinto sect* – consists of those that continue to follow what was taught in ancient prehistoric Shintoism
3. *Confucianism sect* – consists of those who adhere to more to the ethics of Confucianism
4. *Mountain Worship sect* – consists of those who worship the mountains
5. *Purification sect* – consists of those who are specialized in purification rites

Ancient Shinto (Koshinto)

This sect is a reconstructed form of Shinto that existed before the advent of Buddhism. Based on the tenets and principles of Ryukyuan and Ainu practices and religion that are believed to be older than Buddhism, the leaders and followers of Koshinto work on connecting with the spiritual aspects of ancient Shinto before it achieved the written-down structural form. Koshinto is based on beliefs that existed even before the writing system was discovered in Japan and, therefore, it lays more emphasis on kotodama or the speech of the soul or oral traditions.

Chapter 2: Shinto Shrines Basic Introduction and Types

A Shinto shrine, also referred to as a Jinja, is a holy place in which kami reside. In Japan, Shinto places of worship are called shrines, whereas Buddhist places of worship are called temples. However, Shinto shrines are also temples. Every village, town, and community has a local shrine in which the local kami is enshrined and worshipped.

For the Japanese people, shrines are sacred places of calm and peace. Shrines are sources of spiritual vitality and are seen as spiritual homes. Many Japanese citizens visit and pay their respects to the same shrine right through their life. Shrines need not be buildings; they could be trees, rocks, or mountains which manifest special kami characteristics.

A big Jinja could contain many smaller shrines, each dedicated to different kami. The size of Shinto shrines can range from a few square feet to thousands of acres. Many of the shrines are landscaped such that they are connected to the natural world. Therefore, you will find shrines that include sacred streams, tree groves, etc. Sacred structures and symbols such as shimenawa ropes and torii gates are used to separate the holy space of the shrine from the outside world.

While every small village and community has its own shrine dedicated to the local kami, many shrines have a national rather than a local perspective. These national shrines are visited by millions of Japanese, mostly during important annual festivals pertaining to those specific shrines.

Japanese people do not have a specific day of the week or month when they visit shrines. They go whenever they feel like it or on certain festival days. People also visit the local shrine to pray to the local kami for all kinds of favors, including doing well in an exam or for getting a good job or other material needs.

Elements of a Shinto Shrine

Mostly, shrines are made of natural materials, and cypress wood is commonly used to build shrines. Shrines are dedicated to specific kami and are built to provide a home for them. Shrines could contain sub-shrines dedicated to different kami and need not to be dedicated to only one.

While shrines are built for kami, it is not common to see statues of the kami. Many shrines have statues of various animals like the fox or horse. These animal statues are built to honor their service to the kami; they do not represent the kami.

Most shrines have elements designed in such a way that human hands do not overly manipulate the natural aspects of the materials used. The elements are made with as little human intervention as possible. This approach is to emphasize the deep connection between shrines and the natural world. There are gardens in nearly all the shrines, and these are built to create a harmonious and spiritual connection between man and the natural world.

Torii

The entrances to all Shinto Shrines are characterized by the torii which are arches made of two vertical cylindrical pillars connected by two horizontal crossbars at the top. The torii, usually made of wood, are painted either in black, bright red, or orange. This structure is a symbolic gate that separates the ordinary, secular, and profane outside world from the spiritual and sacred realm of the kami.

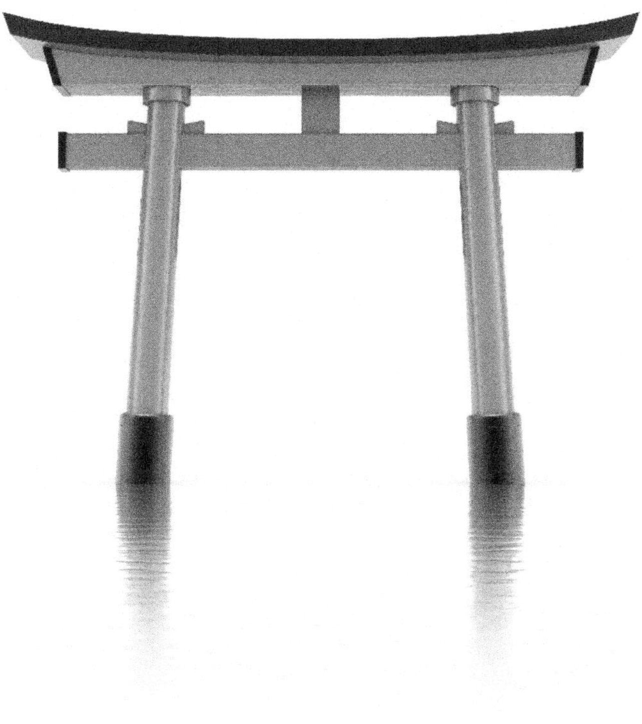

The absence of physical gates means a Shinto Shrine is always open. Torii does not have to be in front of a shrine but can be built to represent or mark an area such as a mountain, stream, or a tree which is a manifest of the kami in that area.

The elements of a torii include the following:

- Hashira - the vertical pillars
- Kasagi – the crossbar lintel placed at the top of the hashira
- Shimaki – a second crossbar below the kasagi
- Nuki –the tie beam, found below the kasagi, that keeps the entire structure together
- Daiwa – a decorative ring found at the top of the hashira
- Gakuzuka – a structure between the kasagi and nuki for added support

Not all the elements mentioned above are found in every torii. The vertical pillars, the single crossbar lintel, and the tie beam are the most basic elements found in all torii. The rest are optional. One of most beautiful torii in Japan is at Fushimi-Inari shrine. The 2 ½-mile path to the main shrine is lined with over 10,000 bright red torii.

Shimenawa

is a rope made of twisted straw and hung between the hashira of the torii. Paper and/or cloth streamers, referred to as Shide, and straw are hung from the shimenawa and can be used to mark off any ritual or sacred areas within the Shinto Shrine. The shimenawa can vary in length; from several meters to just a few centimeters.

More About the Shimenawa

There is a myth associated with Shimenawa. Remember the cave in which the Sun Goddess was sulking after her brother's misbehavior? The other kami joined hands and tricked her into coming out of the cave. After she emerged and was compelled to take her rightful place in the heavens, the shimenawa is believed to have been tied across the mouth of that cave to prevent the Sun Goddess from entering it again.

Shimenawa Izumo Kami instructed people to tie Shimenawa along the roads to keep out diseases.

Irrespective of the story of its origins, the shimenawa is a boundary separating the sacred from the profane, and is used to ward off evil spirits and diseases as well. A shimenawa found tied around a tree or rock is called a Yorishiro and has the power to attract kami. Cutting down trees that have a shimenawa tied around them is considered inauspicious. . The Japanese believe that this Sumo wrestler is actually a living Yorishiro who has a powerful spirit inside of him, so a shimenawa is also used to adorn the highest-ranking Sumo wrestler. A shimenawa is also tied around a place where a sacred ritual, such as ground-breaking ceremony before the construction of a new building, is expected to take place.

The Shimenawa at the Izumo Taisha Shrine is one of the best and the most spectacular shimenawa in Japan.

Komainu

The entrance to a Shinto Shrine could be guarded by a pair of lions or dogs, referred to as Komainu. These statues are kept to ward off evil spirits. There are two kinds of komainu; one is found near the torii and one is found guarding the entrance of the main shrine (or Honden). The komainu standing guard near the torii made of stone is, called sando komainu, and. The other, made of metal or wood stands guard at the entrance of the inner sanctuary and is called jinnai komainu.

Shrine members or important members of the local community donate the komainu. Komainu are guardians welcoming visitors and promising to take them to a place that is free from evil and the malicious spirits of the profane world.

Temizuya

The Shinto followers deeply believe in being pure before presenting themselves before the kami of the shrine. They believe it is wrong to pray when one is impure. Therefore, every Shinto shrine will have a temizuya (or chozuya), which is a purification place containing water troughs along with ladles for visitors to wash their hands and face before walking toward the main sanctuary of the shrine. The concept of purification, or oharai, is the most fundamental aspect of Shintoism.

Honden

is the main sanctuary of the kami and is believed to be the place where the kami of the shrine resides. Only priests are allowed to enter the honden, and visitors have to remain outside. The honden with the enshrined kami is the heart of the Shinto Shrine and is the most sacred space in the shrine.

The roof of the honden is decorated with distinctive wooden ornaments called as katsuogi and chigi. If the chigi is cut horizontally, then the shrine's kami is a female deity, and if it is cut vertically, the kami is a male deity. Similarly, if the kami is female, there will be an even number of katsuogi, and if it is male, there will be an odd number of katsuogi.

Haiden

is a worship hall in the Shinto shrine. In some shrines, there may not be a honden but only a haiden. This happens especially in cases where the kami is a natural feature like a mountain, stream, or tree. In the shrines which have the honden, the haiden will be right in front of it. The visitors usually pray and worship in this hall. The haiden is almost always larger than the honden because it needs to accommodate many visitors.

Heiden

is an offering hall. This hall holds the sacred offerings, referred to as heihaku. The heiden is usually built in continuation of the haiden and the honden and is also a place where rituals are performed in the shrine.

Shintai

There are no statues of the kami in a shrine. Instead, there is an object called shintai which is used to symbolize the kami of the shrine. The shintai could be a man-made object like a mirror or a natural object like a stone. The object is concealed in wrappings; some of the wrappings in many old shrines have been there for centuries. In such cases, no one really knows what the object that symbolizes the kami is. If the shrine is for a natural object such as a waterfall, a mountain, a tree, a rock, etc., then these objects themselves are the shintai. Packaging and wrapping are an essential part of both religious and secular life in Japan.

Heihaku

is a name given to the stick that stands vertically in front of the honden. Streamers hang on this stick, and the heikaku symbolizes the presence of the kami in the honden. Therefore, during processions, the heihaku is also carried around. In some cases, the heihaku is also seen as the shintai of the shrine. Heihaku also refers to the offerings made by the visitors to the shrine.

Types of Shrines

Shinto shrines are categorized into various types based on different factors including but not limited to:

- The kind of architecture used
- The kami which is enshrined inside it
- The sect it belongs to

There is a mind-boggling number of shrine types, so focusing on a few major and popular ones that are accepted by nearly all sects and followers of Shintoism makes sense.

Imperial Shrines

were directly funded and managed by the Imperial Palace when Shinto was the state religion of Japan from the Meiji Period right up to World War II. Many of the large and important shrines in Japan are Imperial Shrines, and some of these include Izumo Shrine, Atsuta Shrine, and Ise Shrine. Imperial Shrine is easily recognizable by its distinctive chrysanthemum crest of the Imperial family. Additionally, Imperial Shrines are not referred to by '*jinja*' but by the less common term '*jingu*.'

Wooden gate, Imperial Seal of Japan

Imperial Shrines or Jingu Shrines are invariably dedicated to Amaterasu, the Sun Goddess, from whom the Imperial Family claims divine descent. Imperial Shrines are also referred to by other names including Imperial House Shinto, Ise Jingu, State Shinto and Koshitso Shinto.

Inari Shrines

enshrine the kami of rice called Inari. Fox (*kitsune*) statues are commonly found in Inari Shrines as komainu. Foxes are believed to be the messengers for Inari Kami. Among the many Inari Shrines found all over the country, the Fushimi Inari Shrine in Kyoto is the most popular and famous one is dating back to 711 A.D.

Fox statue in Kyoto, Japan

Inari are also called by other names including Oinari-sama or Oinari. She is the goddess of rice cultivation, the goddess of five grains, and the goddess of harvest. Her name means 'rice cargo.' She is also connected with the patron deity of grain and agriculture, Uka no Mitama no Kami. Inari shrines are typically characterized by vermillion-colored torii with a fox statue standing guard on either side.

Hachiman Shrines

As the name suggests, Hachiman Shrines are dedicated to the kami of war and were very popular among the warrior clans of Japan in the past. The most famous Hachiman Shrine in the country is Kamakura's Tsurugaoka Hachimangu. Hachiman was actually the highly revered Emperor Ojin who ruled over Japan in the 15th century. After his death, he was deified by warriors as the kami of war.

Tsurugaoka Hachimangu Shrine

Hachiman Shrines are usually dedicated to three deities including Emperor Ojin, his wife Himegami, and his mother, Empress Jingu. Hachiman is the tutelary kami of the famed Minamoto clan, the clan to which the founder of the Kamakura shogunate, Minamoto Yoritomo, belonged. The main Hachiman shrine is the Usa Hachimangu in Ōita Prefecture.

Tenjin Shrines

These shrines are typically dedicated to Sugawara Michizane (who lived between 845 and 903 A.D.), a politician and scholar of the Heian Period, who became a kami after his death. Plum trees and ox statues are characteristic features of Tenjin Shrines.

Michizane is the kami of scholarship, calligraphy, and learning, and for this reason, Tenjin Shrines are frequented by students when they wish to seek divine blessings to clear examinations. Michizane was demoted and sent away from the capital city of Kyoto to Dazaifu, present-day Kyushu, where he died a sad and angry man. After his death, a lot of social unrest occurred in Kyoto which people attributed to being his revenge for the humiliation he suffered. He was raised to kami-hood and since then has been the patron deity of learning.

The top three most revered Tenjin Shrines are:

- Egara Tenjin in Kamakura
- Dazaifu Tenmangu in Fukuoka (where Michizane was exiled to after his demotion)
- Kitano Tenjin in Kyoto (the birthplace of Michizane)

There are Tenjin Shrines dedicated to Emperor Meiji who ruled Japan from 1852 – 1912 A.D.

Kitano Tenjin Shrine in Kyoto, Japan

Sengen Shrines

Enshrined in Sengen Shrines is Princess Konohanasakuya, the kami and Goddess of Mount Fuji. Sengen Shrines are also called Asama Shrines. The name of Princess Konohanasakuya is also spelled as Konohana Sakuya Hime, and in addition to being the patron deity of Mount Fuji, she is also the kami of cherry blossoms. Pregnant women pray for her blessings for an easy and smooth childbirth. Konohana is the daughter of the kami of mountains, Ōyamatsumi. Ninigi, the grandson of the Sun Goddess Amaterasu, was her husband. In one night, she became pregnant and delivered three children who were enveloped in a ring of fire. Some mythological stories say that she died in that fire and, therefore, she is likened to the short-lived cherry trees in bloom. However, other versions say she survived the fire.

One of her children, Hori no Mikoto, married the daughter of the Dragon King, and this union brought forth the first Japanese emperor, Jinmu Tenno. Multiple Sengen Shrines are all over Japan, and the chief one is located at the summit and foot of Mount Fuji.

Shrines of Famous Clan Founders

Oyama Shrine

Multiple powerful clans are all across Japan, and the members of these clans revere their founders as kami and build shrines for them, too. Famous examples of such places of worship include:

- Toshogu Shrines – dedicated to Tokugawa Ieyasu, the powerful warlord of the 16th century- the most famous one is at Nikko
- Oyama Shrine at Kanazawa – dedicated to the founder of the powerful and influential Maeda clan, Maeda Toshiie

Local Shrines

There are multiple shrines in every village, town, and community that enshrine the local kami.

In addition to the above types, shrines are categorized based on the architecture of their honden and some of the best-known ones include:

Shinmei-zukuri

This type of shrine is associated with the architecture used to build rice warehouses. The wood is unpainted and bare, but, gold- and copper-plated hardware is used in this type of shrine and. there are no doors or windows. A classic example of a Shinmei-zukuri shrine is Ise Jingu in Mie Prefecture.

Taisha-zukuri

Based on the homes of village headmen, this kind of shrine is one of the oldest building types in Japan. A characteristic feature of Taisha-zukuri styled shrine is the roof that is built over the steep staircase leading up to the honden. A classic example of a Taisha-zukuri is Izumo Taisha in Shimane Prefecture.

Nagare-zukuri

Translating to 'flowing style,' this type of shrine buildings is the most common type seen all over the country. Stairs on one side and verandas on the other three sides are characteristic features of this kind of shrine architecture.

Kasuga-zukuri

is a little 1 * 1 bay honden with a small stair covered by a pent roof. The walls are white-plastered, and the woodwork is typically lacquered in red. The stair is made as long as the building, and is not restricted to the middle of it.

Sumiyoshi-zukuri

This building type has its origins in the style of temporary ritual palaces built for emperors for their enthronement rituals. A wall with a door for passing through separates the front and rear sections.

Hachiman-zukuri

In this rather unique architectural form, two buildings are parallel and so close that their eaves almost touch each other. Typically, Hachiman-zukuri shrines do not have a separate heiden or offering hall.

Kamidana The Shinto Altar in Japanese Households

Kamidana is a Japanese term that translates to 'god-shelf or kami shelf' which is a miniature shrine found in nearly all Japanese households and business places The kamidana is the center and place of daily worship and displays offerings and articles of veneration.

At the center of a typical kamidana, you will find the taima, or an inscribed board, from the most important Shinto shrine at Ise. The taima represents the universal kami. On either side of the centrally placed taima, you will see a lot of paper amulets or ofuda connected with ancestral spirits and local tutelary gods.

The kamidana at home will also have a shimenawa to demarcate the sacred spot from the profane parts of the home. The offerings kept at the kamidana could include sake (rice beer), water, green twigs, food, etc. and areplaced fresh every day by the members of the family. When placing the offerings, prayers are sent up to the kami for blessings. Other accessories in and around the kamidana include:

Sakaki

two branches of this Japanese evergreen sacred tree are kept on either side of the kamidana.

Sakaki-tate

these are little vases to keep sakaki leaves, the water in these vases is changed daily.

Kagari-bi

is the candle holder which holds small, white candles that are lit during prayer time

Kumo

is nothing more than a piece of paper with the word, kumo (or cloud) written on it and placed above the kamidana. The kumo is a symbol of the highest position that the enshrined kami holds. However, owing to restricted circumstances, the kamidana is not placed high up in the clouds!

Shrines hold a very important place in the life of a Shinto believer and this chapter is only a tip of the iceberg when it comes to types and the criticality of Shinto Shrines. Shinto shrines' architecture, classification, sacred elements, Shinto priesthood, and many other aspects still need to be discussed. Read on for more information about Shinto Shrines.

Chapter 3: Shinto Shrine Sacred Elements, Priesthood, & Architectural Features Specific Details

Sacred Elements in a Shinto Shrine

Every element in a Shinto Shrine has a reason for its existence. Knowing and understanding the purpose for each of the components will help us appreciate a shrine experience in a much better way. Some of the sacred elements in a Shinto Shrine have already been explained in detail in the previous chapter, and therefore, get only a cursory visit here. The others have a detailed explanation.

Torii – The Shrine Gate

Standing as a symbol of purity that separates the profane outside atmosphere from the sacred one within the precincts of a Shinto Shrine, the torii is an unmistakable distinctive Japanese icon.

Sando – The Path of the Worshipper

Also referred to as the 'worshipper's pathway,' the sando leads visitors to the main shrine and extends from the outermost torii right up to the honden. Most shrines have their sando paved with flagstone or gravel. Walking the entire length of the sando is like a pilgrimage for worshippers providing them with a complete tour of the shrine. Visitors should not walk right in the center of the sando because the central axis or seichu is considered to be only for the kami of the shrine but should walk either on the right or left of the pathway.

In the older shrines, large trees line the sando pathway which act as a demarcation through the sacred forest that is also believed to be the home of several kami. When you visit shrines with this kind of sando, picking up even a single fallen leaf from the forest is forbidden. Of course, cutting down trees at such places is absolutely forbidden too. Perhaps, for this reason some of the oldest shrines in Japan exist in the middle of unspoiled and preserved forests for centuries.

Some of the other elements already discussed in the previous chapter are:

Shimenawa – The Sacred Rope

The shimenawa is used to denote the separation of profane and sacred spaces within and outside the shrine.

Temizuya – The Cleansing Place

With water and ladles made available here, worshippers can purify and cleanse themselves before moving on to the main shrine.

Komainu – The Guardian Figures

Found at both the torii as well as the main sanctuary of the kami, the komainu can be figures of foxes (messenger of Kami Inari) or oxen or lions, etc.

Honden, Haiden, and Heiden

The main sanctuary of the kami, the prayer or worship hall, and the offering hall, are found in nearly all shrines as separate rooms or as dedicated spaces in one room.

Shintai – The Divine Object and Shinboku – The Divine Tree

Shintai, or the body of the kami, is located inside the sanctum sanctorum within the honden. This innermost sanctorum is referred to as naijin. The outer part of the honden where the priests perform their rituals is called gejin.

The Shintai, or the sacred objects that represent the kami, are usually mirrors, swords, or comma-shaped stones (magatama). These sacred kami-representing objects are kept safely ensconced in the naijin, and are never displayed or exhibited to the worshippers.

At its most basic form, Shintoism is nature worship, and many shrines reflect this tenet through their shintai. For example, in many shrines, shintai is not a manmade or artificial object, but rather a natural landmark or object, and these objects are referred to by different names.

A sacred mountain is called and worshipped as kannabi. Majestic, unique, or striking rock formations are called iwakura and are worshipped as yorishiro. Large beautiful forest areas are referred to as himorobi, and ancient trees are worshipped as shinboku.

Tamagaki – The Sacred Fence

This sacred fence, or tamagaki, encloses the honden, again, to keep the most sacred part of the shrine separated from the other less sacred parts of the shrine and the profane outside world. Depending on the size of the shrine, multiple tamagaki might be present. When more than one sacred fence exists, then the innermost one is referred to as mizugaki, and the outer fences are called tamagaki, itagaki, or aragaki.

Shamusho – The Shrine Office

The shamusho is a building inside the shrine precincts where the business of the shrine (other than rites and rituals) is conducted. The priests and priestesses relax here and rest when there are no rituals taking place. The Shamusho is also a place where requests for special rites, ceremonies, and prayers are received and recorded.

Visitors may purchase tokens, oracles, and amulets at a public counter. Worshippers say they are 'receiving' these items from the shamusho and not 'buying' them considering the religion they represent is against commercialism. The objects sold at Shinto shrines include:

- ***Shinsatsu*** – amulets that worshippers believe contain the powers and the spirit of the residing kami. Shinsatsu are large talismans that worshippers receive to place them in their kamidana.
- ***Mamori-fuda*** – are small-sized shinsatsu that are designed to be carried on the person
- ***Hamaya*** – translating to 'demon-breaking-arrows,' hamaya are decorative arrows received to ward off evil spirits and other forms of misfortune from homes and shops.
- ***Ema*** - are wooden plaques with a picture on one side and writing space on the other side. Worshippers buy these ema write their prayers, and offer them up to the kami of the shrine to receive blessings.
- ***Omikuji*** – is a small piece of paper which has a fortune written or printed on it. Worshippers draw an omikuji randomly, and the fortune-card they see provides a general prediction of their future.

Shozoku – Shinto Vestments and Shrine Functionaries

Shozoku, distinctive in their style and design, are the traditional garments worn by the Shinto priests and priestesses. . While the original design seems to have its origins in the garments of old Chinese courtiers, during the Heian Reign (794 – 1185 A.D.), it underwent considerable change to incorporate distinctive Japanese elements

These distinctive shozoku are worn only by the priests and priestesses of Shinto Shrines. Initially, these garments were designed for men alone as women were not allowed to enter into Shinto priesthood. However, in recent times, all that has changed, and you will find a lot of female priests conducting rites and rituals as per traditional Shinto practices. Therefore, shozoku are designed for priestesses as well.

There are three classes of Shinto Vestments including:

Seiso (or the formal wear)

Designed in the ikan style, the seiso consists of a colored robe (sometimes with a colored and patterned belt too), referred to as ho, worn over loose trousers called hakama with a headdress called the kanmuri.

Reiso (or the ritual wear)

Reiso vestments are designed in seifuku style wherein the garment is made of pure white cloth with no colors or patterns. These garments are used exclusively by Shinto priests while they conduct rites and rituals. Sometimes, reiso garments are used instead of seiso garments for very formal ceremonies.

Joso (or the ordinary wear)

Also called kariginu, joso vestments are designed to facilitate movement, are everyday garment worn by the priests, and most visitors and worshippers see them in the joso vestment. When priests wear the joso, they also wear a tall hat called eboshi. They do not combine the kanmuri with the joso.

The color of the loose trousers (or hakama) signifies the rank of the priest. The highest ranking priests (gon-guji and guji) wear purple hakama. The lesser ranking priests such as the gon-negi, negi, and others wear the light blue hakama. Shinto vestments also have other accessories including the shaku or a baton (which the priests carry around in their right hand) and asagutsu (or low wooden clogs on their feet).

In addition to priests and priestesses, young and unmarried shrine maidens, called miko, are assistants to the priests, but are not ordained priestesses. The miko wear read hakama.

Shinto Priests

In modern Japan, to serve in Shinto Shrines or become priests and priestesses, one has to pass examinations conducted by Association of Shinto Shrines. Both men and women can take these examinations though until recently, Shinto priesthood was banned for women. Moreover, until recent times, no standardized processes or procedures existed to become a Shinto priest.

Either the Imperial Court appointed Shinto priests, or they followed the priestly lineage. Essentially, the son of a Shinto priest was only allowed to become a Shinto priest. A royal decree abolished the hereditary aspect of Shinto priesthood along with the private ownership of shrines during the Meiji Era. Various ranks are waiting to be awarded to students depending on the level of the course they have taken up. These ranks include:

- ***Jokai*** – This is the highest rank a student of Shinto priesthood can obtain. For this, a student has to put in many, many years of the study and practice of Shinto rites and rituals.
- ***Meikai*** – This is the minimum qualification needed to be the head priest (guji) or assistant priests (gon-guji) of most of the established Shinto Shrines across the country.

- ***Seikai*** – This is the minimum qualification needed to be head priest of a prefecture-level shrine or as low-ranked priests in more prominent shrines.
- ***Gonseikai*** – This is the qualification required to serve as a Shinto priest at town and village-level shrines. Priests holding this rank in priesthood studies will not qualify for high-ranked priests at prefecture-level shrines.
- ***Chokkai*** – This is the most basic entry-level rank for Shinto priesthood.

Job Titles Held by Priests at Most Shrines

- Guji – the chief priest
- Gon-guji – the deputy or assistant priest
- Negi – low-rank priests
- Gon-negi – assistant to low-ranked priests

Job Titles at Ise Jingu Shrine

The Ise Jingu Shrine, or the Grand Shrine of Ise, is, perhaps, the most important Shinto Shrine in Japan and influences Shinto followers and believers in many ways. Its main shrine and sub-shrines are dedicated to:

- Amaterasu Omikami (female, Sun Goddess)
- Toyo-uke Omikami (male, kami of agriculture and industry)

The chief priest and priestess of Ise Shrine are ideally descendants or members of the Imperial family. The worship rites and rituals of the Sun Goddess are particularly important for the Imperial family because they claim direct descent from the goddess. The priestly class at Ise Shrine is, therefore, different from the other shrines. The job titles at the Ise Shrine include:

- Saishu – the highest ranked priest who holds the position of master of religious ceremonies
- Daiguji – high priest or chief priest
- Shoguji – assistant priests
- Gon-negi – lower-ranked priests or deputies of lower-ranked priests
- Gusho – shrine administrators
- Nai-shoten – female attendants who assist the Emperor to perform the annual rituals

Other Important Job Titles in Shrines

- Hafuri – usually a general term used for priests, and typically this title comes after the kannushi and negi
- Kannushi – a generic term to refer to shrine priests, also referred to as saikan

Shinto Priestesses, Miko, Women Attendants

Miko have always served as shrine maidens, shrine virgins, or spirit mediums. Miko were part of all Shinto religious duties either attached to a particular shrine or without any affiliation moving and traveling all over the countryside performing magic and shamanism. In the earlier times, they also served as carriers of divine revelations either from the land of the dead or from the kami.

In modern times, the role of a miko has been relegated to merely assisting the priest and doing menial labor in the shrine including sweeping and cleaning the shrine compound, selling amulets at the shamusho, performing dances, and helping in prayers and rituals. There are no special qualifications to become a miko.

Today, women can train to become Shinto Priestesses. But, there are very few who want to tread this male-dominated path.

Miko and Shamanic Shinto

Shamanic Shinto involves the employment of Miko (women who possess the 'magical' power to receive divine help and messages) to help grieving people get in touch with departed souls of their loved ones. Even today, this practice is prevalent. Additionally, Miko in Shamanic Shinto perform cures as well as organize religious ceremonies and rituals. There are blind female shamans called Itako.

Important Characteristics of a Shinto Shrine

Measurements

These Chinese brought the Japanese a measuring system called shakkan-ho. While Japan adopted the metric system in 1924, the old shakkan-ho system is still used in traditional architecture. Bays, or kens, are used to measure distances in shrines. A bay is the distance between two columns with the actual distance varying according to the custom, age, and location of the shrine.

Wood Construction

The Hinoki Cypress wood proliferates all over Japan and has provided timber both for shrine and temple-building for centuries. The structures of all shrines are made with cuts and joints with very little usage of glue, nails, and other manmade adherents. While many of the older shrines have pillars that go directly into the ground, almost all the shrines built after the 8th century have stone bases for added strength. Walls are made with clay or wooden boards and are plastered over bamboo lath.

Regular Rebuilding

Shinto shrines follow the custom of shikinen sengu which means regular periodic rebuilding of the shrine. The periodic reconstruction is typically fixed for 20 or 21 years though it is highly dependent on the shrine. There are many reasons for rebuilding including:

- Renewal of rituals to maintain the purity of the shrine
- To counter the natural deterioration of wood, especially those shrines with pillars fixed directly into the ground
- To train new carpenters and construction workers on the ancient art and skill of building techniques; it is imperative to pass on knowledge to new people before the passing of the older generation.

The most established shrine that follows this regular rebuilding norm diligently is the famed Ise Jingu, perhaps, the most important Shinto shrine in all of Japan. Today, most of the shrines are protected under the aegis of Important Cultural Properties which does not allow rebuilding and only allows repair and maintenance.

However, the Ise Jingu continues to honor the tradition of rebuilding every 21 years. This rebuilding exercise has been carried on almost uninterrupted since the 7th century. The only time the rebuilding (every 21 years) was stopped happened during a 100-year interval between 15th and 16th centuries. Other than that, of the 125 structures in the precincts of Ise Jingu, some are rebuilt every 21 years while others are rebuilt every 40 years or whenever needed.

Painted or Unpainted

Shrines can be in the painted or unpainted state. Some of them have a polychrome wood finish while some are left unfinished or unpolished. If and when shrines are painted, typically a vermillion red or cinnabar red is used. Toshogu shrines are usually finished with an ornate polychrome finish. Certain styles of shrines are never painted. Prominent such unpainted styles include taisha-zukuri and shinmei-zukuri.

Roof Types

Straw, cypress bark, miscanthus, cedar, or any other wood shingle, or copper tiles   Shrine roofs are always gabled. Key features of the roof of a shrine include:

Chigi and Katsuogi – These two elements on the roof of a shrine are the most distinctive ones that discern a shrine from an ordinary building or even a Buddhist temple. Forked finials support the ridge board of the roof and extend past it to form a V-shape or sit on the ridge to form an X-shape. These forked finials are called the chigi. These forked finials were the remaining part of the roof brace poles that were bound together with ropes in the ancient times.

Today, however, the chigi are typically symbolic additions to the roof. The direction of their cut tells visitors whether the residing kami is male or female. A vertical cut indicates a male, and horizontal cut indicates a female.

Katsuogi are log-like wood pieces that are forged to the roof ridge. Their numbers could typically vary between five or six. However, some shrines have two katsuogi and a few with up to 12 katsuogi. They are so named because they look like dried katsuo bonito, the famed Japanese fish. In the ancient times, these logs were used to weigh down the ridge and also to hold the straw roof in place. But, by the 5th century, katsuogi also became a decorative symbolic element of Shinto shrines.

Chapter 4: Shinto Texts and Scriptures

Until the 7th century, no written record of Japanese history or scriptures existed. Our understanding of Japan prior to this period is based on Chinese texts that recorded the existence of a very close-knit race in the islands of Wa, as Japan was referred to by the Chinese. The Chinese knew of the existence of the Japanese islands but treated them as a distant and insignificant part of the world.

Yet, the written accounts of the Chinese give us reasonably good insight into the history of Japan. As per these written accounts, during the first five centuries, the southern and the central parts of Japan were occupied by many groups of closely related tribes and peoples. Later historical accounts show the growth and development of a kingdom called Yamato and the king of Yamato was referred to as the 'King of Wa' in the Chinese chronicles.

In the 7th century, motivated by the Chinese, the Japanese people also wanted to write down the history of their country. The stories and legends, until then, were only transmitted in oral form.

In Shintoism, two crucial texts, or scriptures, are highly revered. They are:

- The Kojiki
- The Nohin Shoki

These two scriptures contain the mythological background of the entire Shinto religion and practice and help set some kind of historical context to the Japanese islands and its people. In the 7th and 8th century, Emperor Gemmyo decreed that these texts be put into writing which resulted in two volumes: Record of Ancient Matters (or Kojiki) and Chronicles of Japan (Nihon Shoki or Nihongi). Shinto texts are rich in imagery, visual effects, and symbolism.

Before the writings were compiled, the noble families of Japan kept records of their own mythology and genealogy and each of the family records had variations. By the beginning of the 7th century, The Imperial family had a strong desire to compile and create one consistent record, which when completed, would give credence to their divine lineage o.

Around the end of the 7th century, Emperor Temmu became the most ardent advocate towards this cause, and he assigned this rather humongous task to Hiyeda no Are, one of his courtiers. Hiyeda no Are is sometimes referred to as a man and sometimes as a woman. The reason for choosing this particular courtier was for his famed photographic memory. Emperor Temmu died before it was completed.

After nearly two decades, in 711, Emperor Gemmyo restarted that project of his forefather and ordered Yasumaro, a scholar in his court, to compile what was in Are's memory into written form. The project, this time, is believed to have taken only four months.

The Stories and Myths from the Kojiki and the Nihon Shoki

These texts were completed in the year 712 A.D. and are believed to be the oldest extant historical record of Japan. Any student of Japanese history has to learn and master this text. The Kojiki begins in the period of Kamiyo, or the Age of the Gods. Experts divide the Kojiki into three sections:

- The Age of the Gods – mostly mythical in nature
- The Age of the Gods and Men
- The Age of Men – explains the genealogy of the noble families, and therefore, is deeply connected to the history of the country

Even though the Kojiki combines history with myth, the chronology mentioned in this text is quite comprehensive and covers the entire epochs of Japanese culture right from the legends of the prehistoric period up to the 7th century.

The Age of the Gods begins with a silent, lifeless universe. Then, sounds started and began to indicate particle movement throughout this limitless space called the universe. The movement of particles indicated by sound resulted in light, and this light remained on top of the universe. Below this light, a cloud of particles rose and gathered together to form a cloud called Heaven.

Those particles that were not able to rise formed the Earth. When the Earth began to be created, three deities began work on the process of creation. Simultaneously, the Active and Passive essences also came into being. These two essences became the ancestors of all things in the universe.

The next phase is referred to as Seven Generations of the Age of the Gods in which 12 different deities and their stories are chronicled. The 12 gods, or kami, that appeared during this period were:

- Kuninotokotachi
- Toyokumono
- Uhijini & Suhijini
- Tsunoguhi & Ikuguhi
- Ohotonoji & Ohotonobe
- Omodaru & Ayakashikone
- And lastly, Izanagi & Izanami

The first two deities are called hitorigami (do not have a gender) and the next five are male-female pairs.

Kuninotokotachi

Based on the Japanese script, the meaning of this name could translate to either one of the following:

- The birth of Japan in the story of creation
- Japan will exist until eternity

In the Kojiki text, Kuninotokotachi appears as the 6th kami and as a hitorigami whereas, in the Nihon shoki, this kami comes first and as a pure male. He is a kami born with yang but no yin. In the Ise Shrine, Kuninotokotachi is worshipped as one of the kami of Creation.

Toyokumono

The Japanese name translates to a deity of the cloud. This kami comes 7th in Kojiki and as a hitorigami. In Nohin Shoki, Toyokumono appears 3rd and as a male kami.

Uhijini & Suhijini

This is the first male-female pair of kami that make their appearance in both the Kojiki text as well as the Nihon Shoki. Uhijini (for mud) is the male kami, and Suhijini (for sand) is the female kami. The combination of mud and sand seems to tell us that these two kami were created at a time when the earth was not yet firm but was made up of loose sand and mud.

Tsunoguhi & Ikuguhi

Tsunoguhi (for horns) is the male kami and Ikuguhi (for life) is the female kami in this pair. Scholars are of the opinion that the appearance of these two kami was at a time when plants and animals were able to live and grow on earth.

Ohotonoji & Ohotonobe

The *'ji'* in Ohotonoji is believed to represent male, and the *'be'* in Ohotonobe represents the female. This leads scholars to believe that sexuality was created on Earth reflected by the advent of these two kami in the kojiki text.

Omodaru & Ayakashikone

These names are believed to represent completeness and, therefore, could mean a stage in the advent of humankind where man, woman, or the Earth was complete in all respects.

Izanami & Izanagi

These two comprise the final pair of the 12 deities of the Seven Generations of the Age of the Gods. These two kami are prolific creators and create the island of Japan along with human beings and other kami as well.

The Birth of Japan

The celestial kami, residing in Heaven, sent down Izanami (female) and Izanagi (male) to harden the floating masses of land on earth and settle them down. They received a splendid spear called hoko for this task. Standing at the door of Heaven, the two of them stirred the world beneath their feet. After stirring, as they lifted the hoko out from the floating mass, one drop from the spear fell back on earth and hardened itself to form Onogoro Island.

Izanami and Izanagi came down from the heavens and built a large pillar and a big palace on this newly-formed island. They then walked around the pillar and got married to each other. Before the marriage was consummated, Izanagi spoke first calling her husband a handsome man. He responded likewise calling his wife a beautiful woman.

Their first-born was an incomplete child which they abandoned by allowing the child to float away. Their second child also met with the same fate. The two kami then realized that something was not right and decided to take advice from the celestial kami. There, they were told about the mistake (of speaking first) made by Izanami and also given a solution to undo the mistake by rewinding the entire conversation. After that, the children born to Izanami and Izanagi all became the eight islands of Japan which came to be known as the *country of eight great islands*.

Once the islands were completed, Izanami and Izanagi gave birth to multiple kami that are worshipped in Shintoism events today. The last kami to be born to the divine couple was the fire god, Kagutsuchi. Izanami burned his mother as she delivered him and she slipped into Yomi or the land of the dead. The tears of Izanagi as he cries out at the death of his beloved wife all become new kami.

Moreover, he gets so angry at his infant fire god-son to have killed his wife that he beheaded him. The blood of his son on Izanagi's sword became eight kami of mountains and eight warriors or martial kami. The pool of blood that was formed from the dead son's limbs became iron. Although Izanagi followed his beloved wife to the land of Yomi, he couldn't bring her back. Instead, he earned her wrath, and she cursed him that she will take 1000 men every day to the netherworld. Izanagi countered this by saying that he will create 1500 people every day.

Kagutsuchi, the fire god, fathered three children including the Sun Goddess (Amaterasu), the God of Force (or the Impetuous Male), and the Moon Goddess (Tsukiyomi). The Impetuous Male and the Sun Goddess continued the work of creation by biting off pieces of armor, swords, and jewels they wore and blowing them into the wind. This was how the numerous other gods, goddesses, and the rest of the humankind were created.

The First Japanese Emperor, Jinmu, who is believed to have ruled around 660 BCE, is considered to be a direct descendant of the Sun Goddess. Emperor Jinmu was Ninigi's (the Sun Goddess' grandson) grandson. Therefore, all of the Japanese emperors claim divine descent from the Sun Goddess.

The Moon and Sun Goddesses were constantly bickering with each other which led to the birth of day and night because they could never agree on anything. So, they decided never to lay eyes on each other and parted ways permanently resulting in day and night. The mention of the Moon Goddess is more or less restricted to this story alone. The Sun Goddess and the Impetuous Male take the progress of creation forward. However, they too quarreled, and finally, one day, the Sun Goddess was so angry that she locked herself up in a cave plunging the universe (the Central Land of Reed Plains and the Plain of High Heaven) into darkness.

The hundreds of kami panicked at the sight of their dark world and decided to try and appease the angry, sulking Sun Goddess. They took iron from the Heavenly-Metal Mountains, ordered the smith to make a beauteous mirror, and he created an 8ft string with 500 curved jewels. They hung these items along with white and blue offerings on a tree near the cave where the Sun Goddess was hiding.

One of the kami, His Augustness Grand Jewel Ancestor (who was the one who designed the jewelry), then started conducting rituals in favor of the Sun Goddess and began to dance wildly and lustily. The other kami were so amused by the lusty dancing of His Augustness Grand Jewel Ancestor that they started so laughing loudly that the Sun Goddess was intrigued by how they could be so happy despite the deathly darkness engulfing the universe.

When she asked the people outside, they told her that they were so happy and joyous because they had seen another goddess far more beautiful than she was. Her curiosity got the better of her, and the Sun Goddess came out to see what was happening. As she emerged from the cave, she found herself looking at the newly forged mirror and got carried away by the beautiful lady reflected in it. She came out of the cave and there was light again.

The Impetuous Male was banished for his misdeeds. He went to Earth and had no food to eat. He begged for food, and in pity, the Deity Princess of Great Food turned her jewels and other things she was wearing into food for him. However, doubtful about her intentions, and thinking she was going to feed him filth, the Impetuous Male killed her.

After her death, the Deity Producing Wondrous Ancestor ordered that all the useful things from the dead body of the Deity Princess of Great Food be used to spread food and clothing for humanity. Therefore, silkworms came from her head. Rice seeds were created from her eyes, beans from her nose, millets from her ears, barley from her torso, and more.

The Impetuous Male Deity continued to wander all over the earth. One day, he found an old couple crying piteously. When asked about the reason for their sorrow, they replied that a monster serpent of Hoshi which had eight forks came every year to devour each of their eight daughters in turn. Now, only their last daughter was left, and it was time for the monster serpent to arrive and kill her too.

The Impetuous Male decided to help the couple. However, he first ensured that they were ready to marry their eighth daughter to him in return for his help. They readily agreed. Immediately, the Impetuous Male changed the lady into a comb and tucked it into his hair. He now lay in wait for the serpent to come.

A fierce battle took place between the serpent and the Impetuous Male, at the end of which the latter emerge victorious. He cut the serpent into pieces. However, when he tried to cut the middle part of the snake's tail, his sword broke. When he peered into the serpent's body, he found a wondrous great sword which he presented to the gods in heaven. This sword came to be known as the Herb Quelling Great Sword and is one of the Imperial emblems even today.

At last, the Impetuous Male decided to find a permanent place on Earth for his home. He wanted to live in Izumo, but, he came across the land of Suga and found so much purity in his heart when he reached this place that he chose to make Suga his home instead of the land of Izumo. He built a palace in Suga and lived there while his descendants continued to reside in Izumo hoping to get the sovereignty of Japan for the sixth generation descendant.

However, the Sun Goddess was still very angry at her brother for his misbehavior, and therefore, did not want the sovereignty of Japan (or the Central Land of the Reed Plains) to go to his descendants. She sent one of her own grandsons down to earth to rule. To help him in his task, she handed him the mirror and the jewels which were used to make her come out of the cave and the Herb Quelling Great Sword, given to the gods by her brother. These three became the Imperial Family's Regal Symbols.

After getting the Imperial Symbols, the Sun Goddess' chosen grandson came down to Earth and landed on the mountain peak located on the Kyushu Island. Then, the long conflict between the descendants of the Sun Goddess and those of the Impetuous Male began for the kingship of Japan. The conflict ended when the Impetuous Male gave up his temporal powers to his sister's grandson and retained only his spiritual powers.

From the Sun Goddess' grandson, the first Emperor of Japan, Jinmu, was born. This is believed to have happened around 660 BCE thus leading to the story that the Imperial Family of Japan has a divine lineage along with divine approval to rule the land of Japan. These myths are the basis for the three Imperial symbols of power that are prevalent and revered to this very day in Japan. These three Imperial symbols include the mirror, the jewels, and the sword.

The Nihon Shoki is a sequel to the Kojiki, was written with an intention to correct inconsistencies in Kojiki, and was intended to reassert the status and power of certain clans which were omitted from the earlier text. The Kojiki only favored the Yamato clan, and this skewed perspective needed some correction, it seemed. The corrections and additions are believed to be recorded in Nohin Shoki. The myths and stories in Nihon Shoki are more or less the same as the ones in Kojiki though they are narrated from a different perspective.

Chapter 5: Purification in Shintoism

The concept of purification is the core principle of the ancient Shinto faith. While other religions including Buddhism and Confucianism have been allowed to intermingle and seep into Shintoism, the core of this 'way of the gods' is steeped in kami, the spirits of the universe, and is a highly ritual-based religion.

Perhaps, the most important ritual in Shintoism is the concept of purification. The idea of purifying oneself can be traced back to the Shinto myths wherein Izanagi conducted purification rituals after returning from the land of the dead. Until he was cleansed, he suffered a lot of misfortunes and bad luck brought on by the impurities he had collected from the land of the dead.

Purity is the core of Shinto faith. Impurity is anything that separates us from musubi (the harmonizing and creative power) and kami. The elements that make us impure are referred to as tsumi which translates to 'sin' or 'pollution.'

The Shinto faith believes that human beings are not inherently impure. They are actually born in a very pure state because we are all part of the divine soul. However, as we lead our lives, we pick up various impurities along the way. This pollution can be caused by physical impurities, negative energies, diseases, wicked people, and events connected to death.

Impurity can be picked up from and by everyone and everything around us.

Each of us has different kinds of energies vibrating at different levels. Picking up these energies from others is very easy, and this ability helps us feel empathy and sympathy towards people who are undergoing suffering. Many instances in your life occur when you felt absolutely good all day long, and suddenly you meet with someone who says something (not necessarily in any wrong way) that left you feeling awful.

This negative energy you picked up from this person would follow you right through the day, and if powerful enough, it can stay for a long time until you deliberately make an effort to purify yourself from the effects of it. When two people get into a heated argument, the entire environment around the two people will be suffused with their respective negative energies that might have resonated with each other to reach higher levels of negativity than either of the individual's single negativity. Cleansing ourselves from such negativities so that we can be released from their burden is important. Shintoism believes that purification must take place on a regular basis to lead a fulfilling life and to help us come closer to kami. Shinto faith believes is possible to restore the purity of body and mind through personal practices as well as specific Shinto rituals and rites.

Purification Rites

Referred to as Harae, purification rites are the most common rituals regularly performed by Shinto followers. Salt, water, and fire are the chief purifying agents in Shintoism. Shinto priests are expected to follow stringent purification processes before conducting big, public rituals. They should regulate their body and mind through an intense purification period during which time they will bathe in cold water, follow a strict diet, abstain from stimulants, etc.

Elements of purification rites include:

Haraigushi

is a purification wand, or stick, that has flax or white paper streamers attached to one of its ends. The priest conducting the harae ritual waves the haraigushi over the object, person, or place being purified.

Misogi Shugo

is used to talk about purification rituals in general and also to rituals associated with water.

Shubatsu

This purification ritual employs salt as the purification agent. This ritual entails sprinkling salt over worshippers, priests, and the ground to purify it. Even in Sumo wrestling, salt is sprinkled around the ring to keep it safe from impurities.

Oharae – This is a special ceremony referred to as the '*ceremony of great purification*' where the rituals remove the sin and pollution in a large group of people and/or elements. The Oharae takes place once every six months in the Imperial Household and in various shrines with an intention to purify the entire population in a particular geography. Oharae is also performed in companies after a year-end or also to purge impurities left behind by disasters.

The Effects of Harae

There are plenty of positive effects of performing harae or the purification rites as per Shinto faith. The followers of Shinto believe that performing harae have multiple benefits. Some of the positive results are:

- A feeling of peace along with a sense of appreciation of kami and the joy of our own lives
- Improves the ki (or life force) of ourselves and our family members
- To receive the life force of kami in the form of blessings
- To increase the past, present, and future ki in our lives so we feel more optimistic than before and become spiritually aware
- To understand the importance of not being greedy and egoistic and being balanced in our needs and desires
- To raise our spiritual senses and to feel the goodness of kami
- To sharpen the senses as well as the mind
- To revitalize your body, mind, and spirit
- To enhance creativity and positive energy in your life

There are different places and reasons to conduct and follow harae processes.

Temizuya

Required to be done by anyone entering a Shinto Shrine, Temizu is the purification ritual which involves cleansing your hands and mouth with the pure water that is kept the designated sacred water basin called Temizuya, or chozuya, along with a few ladles. This purification ritual ensures all worshippers and visitors to the shrine approach the residing kami with a clean aura and a pure heart.

How to perform the temizu at a Shinto Shrine – The ritual of temizu has to be done even if you have had a shower at home before leaving for the shrine. Worshippers perform the following steps at the temizuya:

- You have to pick up a ladle and draw water in it and wash your left hand first. The cleansed water should fall on the gravel around the water basin and not put back into the water basin.
- Now, transfer the ladle to your left hand and rinse your right hand.
- Take some water in your hand and use it to rinse your mouth ensuring your pour out the rinsed water from your mouth onto the rocks near the water basin. You should not gargle.
- Use the remaining water in the ladle to rinse your left hand again, and tilt the ladle in a vertical position so the water will slide down its handle thereby cleansing it completely for use by the next person.

Haraigushi or Onusa

The priest waves the haraigushi, or the wand (also referred to as onusa), which is a purification rite per Shinto customs. The priest waves the onusa over the object that requires to be purified which could be a person, a place or location, or objects such as cars, bikes, etc. Haraigushi, or onusa, are made with sticks of bamboo or any other wood. Tied to one end of the stick are some shide, which could be either a bunch of unprocessed hemp fiber or zigzagged sacred white paper. The haraigushi purification ritual is typically carried out before an offering is made to the kami, so the negative energies of the people making the offerings and the offering itself are cleansed and eliminated.

The priest bends at a 15-degree angle and gently but briskly waves the haraigushi so the rustling sound from the shide is heard. The waving movement is neither frantic nor very slow, but just enough to create the rustling sound. Also, at the end of each wave, the priest stops momentarily. So he waves the onusa to the left, pauses for a bit, and then waves it to the right, stops momentarily, and so forth.

The Japanese commonly use the Haraigushi purification process for the following situations:

- To purify a new car
- To purify a new plot of land before starting the construction of a home or building; haraigushi process is supposed to help pacify the spirit of the land.

- The haraigushi is also kept in the kamidana to be used in daily prayers.

The Signification of Shide

Shide, when attached to a shimenawa or the rice rope, facilitates the separation of the profane world from the sacred world. The shide on a haraigushi facilitates the conducting of onusa purification process. Shide seems to have come from the word shidesu meaning 'to signify.' So, shide are fundamental elements that signify or mark boundaries.

Shide on a haraigushi is more for 'sweeping' away negative energies and impurities. Similarly, the shide on shimenawa also keep negativities out of the sacred world. The evil energies and spirits get caught in the strips of paper in the shide and lose their negative powers.

The Rustling Sound of Shide – The sweeping of the haraigushi stick evokes a rustling sound from the shide. Praying to the kami through the use of sounds is a common Shinto belief. Whether it is the ringing of a bell kept high up at the gateway to a shrine or clapping while saying your wish or the clicking of knives by Kagura dancers or the rustling sound of the shide, use of certain types of sounds is believed to wake up the kami to hear the worshippers' prayers and requests.

Misogi Shuho

This purification process is referred to when pollutions and sins are 'washed away,' generally through the use of water, though any other natural resource can also be used for the purification process. The Misogi Shuho can be performed in a sea, river, or a waterfall. The Misogi purification process is a technique that promises human beings connect with the natural resources without any mediation.

Origin of Misogi – Izanagi, who along with his wife-sister Izanami, created hundreds of kami and mankind is believed to have conducted the first misogi after his return from Yomi, or the land of the dead. He wanted to wash away the defilement he had picked up while in the World of the Dead. He wanted to wash away all the impurities and pollutants from his body and mind and make himself an august and pure entity again.

Before he entered the Tachibana River for the misogi purification process, Izanagi got rid of all his possessions. He first threw away his staff and the kami of the Way, Sarutahikono-O-Kami was created from it. He threw away his garments, his jewelry, and everything else he possessed into the river. The articles he got rid of during the misogi process all turned into 12 kami who protect the 12 directions.

Then, he found a spot in the river which was neither too muddy nor too swift. He entered the river at this spot to purify himself. During this misogi, many wrongdoing kami as well as kami to counter the wrongdoing came into being. The followers of Shintoism believe that Misogi Shuho teaches us many things including:

- How to live each day fully
- How to pray sincerely
- How to make the right choices in life and find the right livelihood
- How to work to benefit humanity and the world
- How to rid our body and mind of tsumi
- How to pray for the health and happiness of our families
- How to get through difficult phases

How to solve all our problemsConnecting your mind and spirit with that of kami is possible through the misogi shuho purification process.

Shubatsu

Salt is the cleansing material used in the Shubatsu purification process. Salt is sprinkled in front of homes, restaurants, and offices to ward off evil spirits and to attract the good ones. The shubhatsu has three elements in its purification process:

- Reciting an incantation
- The Onusa or haraigushi
- Saltwater or salt

In fact, salt is sprinkled on people after a funeral ceremony to keep the impurities of association with the dead at bay.

Shrine Ritual Purification

Twice a year, in June and December, Shinto shrines across the country perform a shrine purification ritual to cleanse the impurities accumulated in the shrine as well as to help its parishioners rid themselves of tsumi that have polluted their bodies and minds in the last six months. The two shrine purification rites include:

- Nagoshi-no-Oharahi Taisai - Great Mid-Year Purification
- Oharahishiki - Great Day of Purifying the Root of Misfortune

Nagoshi-no-Oharahi Taisai - Great Mid-Year Purification

Also referred to as Summer Purification Rites, the Nagoshi-no-Obarahi is one of the oldest religious festivals in Japan, dating. Back to the 8th century, probably established during the Nara Reign between 710 and 794 A.D. In those times, this ritual was performed at the shrines as well as at the Imperial Court. However, it was stopped by whom? At the Imperial Court during the Onin War which lasted from 1467 to 1477, but the rite continued to flourish in all Shinto Shrines of Japan.

The Nagoshi-no-Oharahi has its roots in the legend of the Impetuous Male, Susanoo, who was wandering on Earth after being banished from heaven. During his travels, he met a poor man, Somin Shorai, and begged to stay for one night at his house. The poor man showed him every luxury that he could offer to the disguised kami. In return for his kindness, Susanoo gave Somin a chinowa, a wreath woven from reeds. The god told him to wear it for protection.

And true to its protective nature, Somin, his family members, and his descendants escaped the deadly plague and illness that was spreading in his town. This story is the origin behind passing through the chinowa to ward off misfortunes and evil spirits.

Heian Jingu Shrine Chinowa Kuguri Wreath Door

There are many rituals that individuals participate in during this time including:

- Stepping through a big reed hoop called chinowa – the chief priest of the shrine typically leads the parishioners through the chinowa; the passing through the loop has to be done in the form of infinity - ∞ - starting from the right and circling back through the left; the chinowa wreaths are usually placed under the torii or in front of the haiden.
- Holding a doll received from the shrine
- Eating minazuki which is a simple rice cake topped with sweet beans

These rites are believed to help the worshippers cleanse themselves of accumulated impurities and tsumi as well as ward off evil spirits that could bring sickness and other misfortunes.

Oharahishiki - Great Day of Purifying the Root of Misfortune

takes place at the year end and includes rituals and rites that are designed to bring in the New Year in a pure and cleansed form. Shinto prayer, or norito, are read by the priests, and other purification rituals take place in the shrine. Worshippers come in hordes to participate in the purification rituals and be blessed by the kami.

Most of the shrine festivals follow the given order of events:

- Purification rite – takes place before the event begins
- Adoration – is bowing in respectful prayer in front of the altar
- The main sanctuary in which the kami resides is opened
- Food offerings are presented; meat offerings are not allowed to be given
- Prayers – many of which date back to the 10th century
- Music and dance
- Other offerings such as twigs of a sacred tree or paper streamers with prayers
- Removal of the offerings from the sanctuary
- Closure of the sanctuary
- Final Adoration
- A ceremonial meal which invariably includes ritual sake drinking

Chapter 6: Ichirei Shikon, Death, After-Life, and Funeral Customs

Metaphysics plays an important role in every religion, including Shintoism. Shintoism believes that every element, whether place, animal, person, or thing or whether living or non-living, has a soul. This soul can be divided into four distinct parts or spirits including:

- Negi-mitama or the harmonious soul
- Ara-mitama or the harsh soul
- Saki-mitama or the happy soul
- Kushi-mitama or the wondrous soul

While the soul consists of all the above four spirits, or parts, external factors decide which spirit is dominant in a particular state. The phenomenon of one soul, four spirits in Shintoism is called Ichirei Shikon. Let us look at each of the four distinct parts in a bit of detail.

Negi-Mitama or the Harmonious Soul

The negi-mitama is the natural state of the soul. This form is dominant when the external environment around the soul is relaxed, calm, and peaceful. When the soul exhibits this aspect, then there is natural and straightforward affection and love towards everyone and everything.

The negi-mitama is a crucial part of the soul which when working well creates harmonious relationships with everyone. The dominance of this spirit of the soul creates selflessness and magnanimity resulting in improved social skills for the person concerned. The power of this spirit lies in its ability to unify and harmonize the environment and everything in it.

Many shrines have their primary kami enshrined in a separate shrine in the negi-mitama state. So, in certain shrines dedicated to the Sun Goddess, you will find a separate space in which her negi-mitama aspect is enshrined.

Ara-Mitama or the Harsh Soul

The ara-mitama is the counterpart of the negi-mitama, and this aspect is dominant by a violent and savage instinct. Most people will tap into this spirit of the soul when challenged by adversities or problems in their lives. Shinto followers believe that moderating this aspect of the soul is important for creating the right balance in their lives.

Being excessively harsh and violent, even during adversities, will result in a person being perceived as oppressive and having a hurtful behavior towards others. During the dominance of ara-mitama aspect, you may see others from an egotistical perspective and being aware of this will help you moderate yourself in a better way.

Saki-Mitama or the Happy Soul

This aspect of the soul is typically connected with good luck and prosperity. Some people believe this is a subdivision of the negi-mitama. When the negi-mitama is dominant, then this spiritual aspect of the soul also comes to the forefront.

The Happy Soul spreads love, affection, and benevolence to the universe and for all creation. The absence or minimal functioning of this aspect of the soul results in an individual losing his or her humanity. The Saki-mitama spirit looks for joy and happiness in every little element of life and the universe. This approach will help individuals feel an abundance of good emotions and help them live harmonious and happy lives.

Kushi-Mitama or the Wondrous SoulThis spiritual form of the soul is believed to be the counterpart of the Happy Soul and in fact, is considered to be prosperity itself. When the wondrous soul is in a powerful state, then the individual remains in a state of wisdom, opening the mind's eyes, helping us see the wonder of the universe and mankind, and understand things beyond the superficial which, in turn, helps us overcome biased perspectives, and see everything for what it truly is.

The belief of Ichirei Shikon creates a rather complex form of karma or cause and effect. The most crucial duty of a person is to live a dignified and harmonious life so that he or she leaves behind a positive spirit. But, if a person lives a life of dishonor and malice, then the ara-mitama is left behind bringing misfortune and ill-luck for everyone. Now, every living person must return the ara-mitama to negi-mitama which can be achieved through sacrifice and humility (the state of a pure soul).

Shinto followers strongly believe that a pure soul is easily capable of breaking into these four different spirits if prescribed rites and rituals are not performed. Moreover, Shintoism believes that 'evil' is a part of the soul and needs to be managed and eliminated. The concept of the 'Enemy Within' is formed from this idea which has to be destroyed to achieve peace and happiness. No real external evil or pure evil spirits exist. Evil is only the darker side of the soul and can be amalgamated with the good side of the soul.

Death and Mourning

Shintoism treats death as dark, negative, and impure. The myths and legends in the Kojiki and Nihon Shoki talk about the land of the dead, or Yomi, to be a dark realm existing deep underground with a river separating it from the land of the living. Birth in Shintoism is merely the appearance of the soul from the invisible to the visible world, and death is nothing but a reversal of this phenomenon.

Shintoism's primary goal is to achieve immortality among the ancestral beings or in the otherworld of Kami. Believers think an individual's kami survives death. Fulfillment of duty is the ultimate Shinto goal because through the fulfillment of duty, impurity is avoided and purity is retained and enhanced so the surviving kami nature of the dead person is remembered with respect and dignity. A unique tradition is followed in Shintoism. When a child is born, the family adds the name of this newborn to a list maintained in the local shrine. This addition of the child's name is announcing him or her as the 'family child,' or ujiko. After the death of this person, the ujiko changes from 'family child' to 'family spirit,' or ujigami. Children who die before their names are added to the list become 'mizuko,' or water children and are believed to bring bad luck and misfortune. Mizuko are also worshipped in shrines to still and calm their anger which is referred to as mizuko kuyo.

As per the traditional Shinto faith, the concept of death is not really discussed or debated. The influence of Buddhism has incorporated the concept of meditating on death into Shintoism. Meditating on death is believed to help followers understand and appreciate that life on Earth is short and temporary. Thinking of death should act as a challenge to make life on Earth more meaningful and fulfilling.

Mourning in Shintoism is considered and accepted to be a natural human reaction. Intense expression of sadness and grief is, therefore, allowed at funerals on a day that is specified for this kind of open display. At all other times, grief has to be displayed in a controlled and subdued manner, almost stoically. This kind of stoic reaction from mourners is believed to exhibit the high regard and regard respect that one had for the dead person.

After-Life

The Shinto faith believes that the human spirit continues to live forever just like kami with no concept of rebirth or reincarnation. Moreover, death is not a result of the accumulation of sins, but rather the opposite of pure. Shinto believes in three vital forms of impurity including sickness, blood, and death. Offended kami can create disasters resulting in death and destruction, soShinto Shrines do not conduct funerals.

Even if believers feel death is impure, Shintoism has been thinking and dealing with death in different ways. The Shinto faith believes that after death, the spirits go to any of the following four other-world spaces:

The mountains

The concept of dead spirits living in the mountains could be based on the fact that most Shinto cemeteries are on hills that present a panoramic view of the villages. This belief is based on the idea of Shintoism that the dead spirits desire to see their descendants even after they are gone.

Above the sky or Takamano-hara

This is the place where the most venerable living members go after their death. Also referred to as the place where the kami live, the most respected dead spirits also find their way to this place.

Below the earth or the Yomi

is the place where Izanami, the female parent of Japan and its inhabitants, lives. Some believe that spirits of the dead who are buried find their way into Yomi.

Beyond the horizon

This place is somewhere far beyond the horizon of the sea.

Myths of the Yomi

Here, it makes sense to talk about the story of the first death on Earth, the death of Izanami who died of horrible burns while delivering the kami of fire. Her beloved husband, Izanagi, buried her on Mt. Hiba. Izanami's spirit found its way to the land of the dead or Yomi-no-kuni, the underworld.

However, on Earth, Izanagi missed his beloved wife so much that he decided to take a trip to Yomi to see if he could bring her back to the land of the living. She came to meet him at the gate, and Izanagi entreated his wife to return because their task of creation was still unfinished. Izanami responded to this by saying that he was too late in coming as she had already partaken of the food of Yomi, and so she is doomed to remain there forever although she also wanted to return with him.

But, after thinking for a while, she told her husband to stay and wait patiently while she tried reasoning with the lord of the underworld if he can let her go back. Izanagi agreed to wait for her patiently. Soon, however, he lost his patience and breaking off one of his teeth, Izanagi made a torch by attaching it to a comb that was stuck in his hair. With the light from this torch, he entered the land of the dead.

He searched high and low for Izanami and finally found her in a terrible state. Her body was ridden with maggots, and it was rotting. Eight of the most hideous-looking gods were hanging on to her rotting body. Terrified at this ghastly sight of his wife's body, Izanami decided to run away and escape back to the land of the living. However, his wife was furious that her husband broke his promise and saw her in this horrific state. She decided to keep him back in Yomi. She ordered the evil witches under her control to chase him and bring him back to her. This has already been told. Why repeat it? Again, the earlier time was in a brief way and there is a reference there of more detailed information available in this chapter

But, of course, he escaped to the land of the living by blocking the entrance with a huge boulder, thereby permanently separating the land of the dead from the land of the living. He later performed purifying ablutions to rid himself of the impurities of death associated with the land of the dead.

Today, the entrance to the Yomi is believed to be in Matsue, the capital of Shimane Prefecture.Secluded and very quiet, the gloom of the place seems appropriate for it to be taken as the realm that divides the lands of the dead and the living. Another legend associated with Yomi involves Susanoo, the Storm God, and Okuninushi, one of the descendants of Susanoo. When Izanami passed away, Susanoo showed excessive grief and therefore, was banished to live near the entrance of the land of the dead. He built himself a palace and was living there.

One day, Okuninushi came to visit his ancestor seeking help and advice on how to manage his 80 brothers who were troubling him.

When he came to Susanoo's palace, he was attracted to Suseri-hime, the daughter of the Storm God. She fell in love with him too, and they got married. Susanoo was, of course, angry that they married without his permission, and sent a fearsome test for his son-in-law. He had to spend an entire night in a room full of bees, snakes, centipedes, and other crawly, creepy creatures associated with the netherworld. But, Okuninushi's newly-wedded wife helped him, and he came through the test unscathed.

Next, Susanoo ordered his son-in-law to comb his hair and clean the lice from it, as punishment for marrying his daughter without his permission. His son-in-law agreed. But, when he tried to comb his father-in-law's hair, he found poisonous centipedes crawling instead of harmless lice. Again, his wife came to his rescue. She gave him red clay and nuts so that he could chew them, spit them out, and act like he was killing the lice in Susanoo's hair.

Then, when the Storm God was asleep, Okuninushi tied his hair with the lethal centipedes to a raft, and he escaped with his newly-wedded wife. He also stole Susanoo's sword and arrow with which he was able to destroy his 80 brothers and make himself the Emperor of Japan (or the world). This reign lasted until the Sun Goddess, Amaterasu, sent her grandson, Ninigi, down to rule over Japan.

Kami and various supernatural beings also reside in these otherworld places. These places are neither as perfect as Utopia nor as horrible as Hell. In fact, there is not much difference between our real-world and the other worlds where the spirits of the dead live. This approach to death and afterlife reflects a faith that spirits from the otherworlds can visit us when we conduct rites and rituals to revere them, especially during special days such as festivals.

Another belief of Shintoism concerning spirits of our ancestors is that like kami, they work to protect their descendants, provided their family members continue to hold festivals and honor the ancestors and kami.

The Obon Festival

is one such festival that is celebrated around July-August to appease and revere the spirits of ancestors and. Reflects the Japanese people's way of revering and paying homage to their ancestors. After a certain period of time, the spirits of their ancestors become kami which remain forever on our land to oversee and protect their descendants and their family.

The ancestral spirits are enshrined in many places including the place where they died, in cemeteries, in shrines after they become kami, and also in the altars at home. The spirits of the beloved dead watch over the living descendants as they revere and perform rituals and conduct festivals in their honor. Even in today's Japanese custom, after a person is dead, his or her memorial day is celebrated and not the birthday.

Another Shinto custom of afterlife is as follows: A few decades after an individual has passed away, their memorial tablet is replaced with small pebbles which are collected and kept together. The pebble collection becomes the family guardian. The throwing away and replacement of the memorial tablet seems to suggest that the Shinto faith believes in some kind of disconnection that takes place between the ancestral spirit and their descendants.

Funeral Customs

Deaths and funerals are considered impure in Shintoism and in stark contrast to the purity associated with Shinto shrines, so cemeteries are not built close to Shinto Shrines which are considered places of great purity. Again, because of the impure concept of death, Shinto followers abstain from visiting people who are on their deathbeds. Even preparation of the body after death is left to professionals today. Shinto followers have adopted Buddhist funeral customs. A common adage in Japan is, 'shrines for weddings, temples for funerals.' Funeral customs are quiet and simple and are intended to give succor and solace to the surviving members of the family, and dignity and respect for the dead person. The funeral service is performed to create a positive atmosphere for the spirit of the dead to be able to move to the otherworld as smoothly and seamlessly as possible.

When there is a death in the family, the altars at home are closed to ensure the spirits of the dead cannot get in. The eldest son, or the oldest living male member of the family, typically makes the funeral arrangement. The funeral is usually kept as early as possible after death. The only exceptions are made if close relatives need to travel from afar. Also, in the six-day lunar cycle, funerals are not allowed on the second day. All other days are acceptable for funerals to take place.

There are purification rites and rituals for the seamless passage of the dead person's spirit to the other world and also to decontaminate the home of the impurities accumulated from death. The first step is to wash the lips of the dead person which is a symbol of letting the person having his or her final taste of water. Then, the corpse is washed and cleansed with water. Then, the death of the person is announced to the spirit world through prayers and creating memorial tablets at the family shrine. Then, the head is propped up using a pillow, facing north. At this stage, food offerings are made to the kami. A knife or a sword is also placed next to the dead body.

The decorated and cleansed body is now placed in a coffin, and food offerings are given to the deceased. These food offerings are made twice each day until the dead spirit reaches the final resting place. Now, an announcement is made of the dead spirit returning to the shrine, and this happens by simply calling the local shrine and informing them about the person's death.

The next step is to purify the earth at the place where the burial will take place. The priest uses water and prayers for the purification purpose. Next, the priest conducting the funeral ceremony purifies himself. The wake ceremony follows where the mourners gather and express grief and sorrow for the loss. Now, the priest performs a ritual wherein the spirit is transferred from the dead person to a tablet. At this point, food prepared at a different location is served to the mourners.

The funeral service follows consisting of purifying the room where the service is going to take place, prayers for the dead, and eulogies. Next, the farewell ceremony takes place where the mourners walk past the dead person in a single file. This is the ceremony of the final goodbye to the deceased. The coffin is then prepared to be taken to the burial site and carried in a procession.

Next, the home of the deceased person is purified through rituals and prayers. The house is cleansed after the body has been taken away to the burial site. Close family members then gather at the burial site or the crematorium. Offerings made to the dead person are placed inside the coffin, and the body is cremated. There are very few Shinto followers who are buried. Burial is usually restricted to the elite and influential people only.

Then, the bones from the cremation ash are collected and placed in a vase, and the mourners return home with the ash and some bits of the bones which are kept above ground in a mausoleum.

The primary intention of a funeral ceremony in Shintoism is to allow the smooth passage of the dead spirit to the underworld, and to purify the home, other areas of the survivors, and the survivors themselves of the impurities of death. Once the person is dead, then he or she becomes a family spirit and joins the list of ancestors who are worshipped and honored regularly. They, in turn, protect their descendants for eternity.

Chapter Seven: Shinto Festivals and Other Shinto Rituals

Matsuri, or Japanese Shinto festivals, can refer to any occasion in which praise or thanksgiving is offered to a deity. The term comes from a word that means 'to serve' or 'to entertain.' Shinto festivals are a perfect combination of solemn rituals and happy celebrations.

Shinto festivals typically revolve around one particular kami who becomes the god of honor or chief guest at that festival. Celebrations include a lot of physical events including drama performances, processions, sumo wrestling, and of course, feasting. Shinto festivals are loud (sometimes even loutish and vulgar), colorful, aromatic, and bright. These performance elements are always connected to some sensual and/or aesthetic appeal of the shrine, the kami, and their stories.

Processions at a matsuri invariably include a mikoshi, or a divine palanquin, that is used to carry the kami (or the image or a representation of the kami). Mikoshi is also called as a portable shrine or altar. The procession represents a reverse trend wherein instead of the worshipper visiting the shrine to receive blessings from the kami, the kami visits his or her worshippers to bestow blessings.

Many of the Shinto festivals are celebrated around farming seasons because of the connection of the religion to the agricultural prehistory of the country. Today, there are other festivals added to the celebrations that happen all year round with many of them being declared a national holiday. All festivals are typically divided into three segments including:

Kami Mukae (or Kami Mukae Sai)

This term translates to 'welcoming the kami.' At the start of the festival, shrines perform a ritual wherein the kami and the gods are welcomed to Earth.

Shinko (or Shinkosai)

This is the main festival event. The term translates to 'sacred procession' or 'procession of the kami.' The mikoshi, or the divine palanquin, is carried around the streets of the town or within the precincts of the shrine. The kami or a representation of the kami is enshrined within the mikoshi. The procession is an opportunity for the kami to tour their territory. The Shinko has various other names including Shinko-shiki, miyuki, and gyoko.

Kami Okuri

translates to 'sending the kami back.' The ritual of kami okuri is one where the kami is sent back to his or her heavenly abodes, and respectfully so. No festival is complete without this ritual because if the kami is not sent back home in a dignified manner, then he or she can wreak havoc on the community and its people by sending ill-luck and misfortune.Some of the festivals and events are community events, and some of them are personal events or festivals celebrated by families and individuals.

Daijosi or the Great Food Festival

Very rare. Celebrated only once in the lifetime of an emperor, this festival is the extremely elaborate version of the annual ninnemesai, or the annual rice-tasting festival, in which the emperor offers the first harvest of rice to the ancestors and kami before eating it himself. The first ninnemesai performed by an emperor is called the Daijosi, and is part of the enthronement activities and ceremonies.

The annual harvest festival as well as the rarer and more elaborate version, daijosi, was mentioned in both the sacred texts of Shintoism- Kojiki and Nihon Shoki. However, the word 'daijou' made its first appearance during the reign of Emperor Tenmu. The Great Food Festival is mentioned in other important Shinto texts of the 8th, 9th, and 10th centuries.

Dosojin Matsuri

The popular fire festival in Japan is celebrated in mid-January every year. Shrine ornaments such as talismans, decorations, etc used for the New Year are collected and burned in bonfires made of straw, bamboo, and branches of trees. These bonfires are lit with a wish and prayers for a good harvest, prosperity, and good luck in the coming year.

The bonfire made out of burning shrine decorations and talismans has many names such as Dondo Yaki, Sai-no-Kami, and Sagicho. The crackling sound heard from the bonfire can be used to tell how the coming year will be. Children throw their calligraphy work into the bonfire, and if it rises high into the sky, then the children believe they will become good calligraphers.

Additionally, Dosojin is also a folk deity tasked with protecting village boundaries, mountain crosses, and crossroads. This deity has the power to block the pathway of evil spirits that spirit misfortune and diseases. Dosojin is connected to fertility as well. Her statues are found all over Japan.

The Dosojin Fire Festival at Nozawa is one of the most famous ones in Japan,. dating back to 1863, and is held every year in mid-January. The purpose of the festival is for believers to pray for an abundant harvest, good fortune, and good health. Nozawa Onsen is located in the Eastern Alps of Nagano Prefecture and is a four-hour drive from Tokyo.

The Nozawa Dosojin Festival features snow, fire, and sake along with colorful, gay parades, processions, and ceremonies conducted at the village square. A vast wooden shrine made of natural flammable materials such as wood and rice stalk is built for the bonfire. . The entire process of building this wooden shrine for the Dosojin Festival is undertaken by about 100 villagers each year. When the shrine is ready, the priest from the village's Kosuge Shrine performs a ritual through which the kami of dosojin, the local deity is installed in it.

Now, starts the battle. There are two opposing teams; one offensive team is pitching to set the shrine on fire, and the other defensive team striving to save the shrine from being turned to cinder. The team pitching to set the shrine alight carries fire torches, and the team pitching to save it sits at the base working out ways and means to douse the fire. Team is a collective noun, which is singular, so it needs singular verbs

The defensive team consists of two teams of 25-year-old men and 40-year-old men. These men are chosen based on a Shinto belief that these ages are unlucky, and therefore, the men going through these ages (referred to as yakudoshi) must be purified through rituals. Participating in the Dosojin Festival is a way of purification.

The finale of the event is a blazing bonfire through which prayers and wishes are sent up to the kami for a good fortune and happiness in the coming year.

Kekkonshiki (Weddings)

Nearly all Japanese weddings are based on Shinto rituals, and new couples take vows before the kami. While the weddings take place in elaborately decorated and grand halls, there will always be a temporary shrine altar erected to take vows in front of the kami. A Shinto priest presides over the wedding rituals and ceremonies. He recites prayers (or norito) spoken in an archaic form of the Japanese language.

The San-san-kudo, which translated to three-three-nine-times, is a unique Shinto wedding feature which is a ritualized way of drinking sake as a couple to solemnize a marriage. Many times, the parents of the couple are also included in the ritual to increase bonding between the families, though this is frowned upon by the old purists.

Three ceremonial sake cups called sakazuiki are stacked one above the other. The couple sips from each cup in turn three times, hence the ritual is called three nine times. As three cannot be divided into two, it is a particularly lucky number for Shinto weddings. Many explanations are given for this symbolic wedding ceremony. Some people believe that the three cups represent mankind, Heaven, and Earth. Some others believe that they represent happiness, love, and wisdom which grow slowly but surely over time in a marriage. Some more believe that the three cups represent the three human weaknesses of ignorance, hatred, and passion.

Hatsumode

The literal meaning of the term hatsumode is '*to pay the first shrine visit in a new year*.' Worshippers use this first shrine visit in a new year to thank the kami for the blessings received in the past year and pray to the kami for good health and good fortune for the upcoming year. Ideally, on this day, the Shinto priest presents a short sermon and welcomes all worshippers to share a cup of sake. Bonfires are also lit on this day. Even if some of the people cannot come on the formal day of Hatsumode, they make it a point to visit the shrine on some day in early January for thanksgiving and prayers for continued patronage and protection from the kami.

Miyamairi

This ritual is for baptisms and christenings of newborn babies. One month after a baby is born (typically 30 days for boys, and 32 days for girls), the family takes the baby for a visit to the shrine to express thanks, and to pray to the kami for the baby's health and happiness. A Shinto priest (or kannushi) oversees the Shinto baptism ceremony in which the priest recites the norito and swings the tamagushi (or haraigushi) from right to left to purify the baby.

During the norito incantation, the priest says the name and the birthday of the baby. Then, the baby is taken to the altar, and the parents bow before it holding the baby in their arms. After this, the baby is fed sake in a red wooden cup.

The Most Popular Shinto Festivals in Japan

Kanda Matsuri held at Kanda Myojin Shrine (Tokyo)

During the Edo Period, Kanda was a central and important district in Tokyo and continues to hold a place of prominence in Japan even today. Kanda Matsuri is easily one of the top three Shinto festivals of Japan. This festival is conducted in odd-numbered years only and is alternated with the Sanno Matsuri held in even-numbered years only.

Kanda Shrine, Japan

The Kanda Matsuri lasts a whole week while the main procession or parade takes place on a Saturday that is closest to May 15th. More than 300 people carry over 100 mikoshis through the streets of Kanda on this main parade day.

The Kanda Matsuri started as a festival to celebrate the victory of Tokugawa Ieyasu in the Sekigahara Battle then was continued to exhibit the show of pomp and splendor of the Edo Court. Today, this festival is celebrated to pray for the prosperity of the residents of Kanda. A multitude of mikoshi, priests on horseback, musicians, and dancers make their way through Tokyo streets with the kami enshrined in the mikoshi blessing the local onlookers. The parade finishes at the Kanda Myojin Shrine.

Sanja Matsuri held at Asakusa Shrine, Tokyo

Another grand and rather boisterous matsuri held on the third Sunday of May, this festival includes the preceding Saturday and Friday as well. Asakusa is the old-fashioned part of Tokyo. This festival attracts over 2 million visitors each year, and therefore, is considered to be the largest matsuri in Japan.

Sensoji-ji Red Japanese Temple in Asakusa, Tokyo, Japan

The Sanja Matsuri is held in honor of the three founding members of the Senso-ji Temple. These three kami are enshrined in the Asakusa Shrine that is next door to the Senso-ji Temple. The festival is quite famous for its raucousness, and the streets are full of musicians, people chanting, and drummers. On the last day of the festival, three mikoshis each carrying a kami of three founding members are taken on a procession at the end of which the kami are laid back to rest in the Asakusa Shrine. The more the mikoshi is shaken, the more good luck will be bestowed on the people.

Aoi Matsuri held at Kamigamo Shrine, Kyoto

The procession for the Aoi Matsuri, also referred to as Kamo Matsuri, starts from the Imperial Palace and ends at the Kamo Shrine in northern Kyoto. Participants wear costumes from the Heian Period and move with the procession either on horseback or on foot. Heian court music plays through the journey.

Although all elements of this matsuri have a Heian background, the Aoi Matsuri predates the Heian period and goes back as early as the 6th century. Emperor Kinmei made offerings to the Kamo Shrine to ward off disasters and disease in his kingdom. During the Heian period, this festival seems to have reached its peak.

Kamigamo Shrine, Kyoto, Japan

In the present day, the Kamo Matsuri starts from the Kyoto Imperial Palace at 10:30 am and reaches the Kamo Shrine at 3:30 pm. The parade, equestrian events, and races are the highlights of the Aoi Matsuri.

Gion Matsuri held at Yasaka Shrine, Kyoto

The Yasaka Shrine is one of the oldest Shinto shrines in Japan. With a 1350-year history, the Yasaka Shrine, or the Gion-Sha, is dedicated to the Storm God, Susanoo, and his wife Kushiinada-hime, and their eight children.

Yasaka Shrine, Kyoto, Japan

The Gion Matsuri is held throughout the month of July with the main festivities occurring on July 17th (Yamaboko Junko) and the three evenings (referred to as yoiyama evenings) preceding it. Yamaboko typically refers to the two types of floats that participate in the Gion Matsuri; the small yama floats, and the large hoko floats. These floats are decorated elaborately with beautiful paper lanterns and tapestries. Some of the large hoko floats need more than 40 people to pull them through the streets of Kyoto.

Although the Gion Matsuri started off as a purification ritual, the merchants and traders of the city starting using it as means to show off their wealth and ostentatious lifestyle. Even to this day, Kyoto homes are open to the public during the Gion Matsuri allowing visitors to catch a glimpse of rare and precious family heirlooms. On July 24th, another less elaborate float festival takes place along with the three preceding yoiyama evenings.

Takayama Matsuri held at the Hei Shrine, Takayama

The Spring Festival held on April 14th and 15th is an annual event at the Hei Shrine which is also known as Sanno-sama. Therefore, the Spring Festival at Takayama is called Sanno Matsuri, too.

Similarly, there is an Autumn Festival celebrated at the Hei Shrine on October 9th – 10th. This festival is dedicated to the Hachiman Shrine in Takayama. The Spring Festival is to pray for a good crop, and the Autumn Festival is for thanksgiving.

Both these festivals at Takayama have similar events and ceremonies. There are festival floats called yatai (yatai is also a term to refer to street food during a matsuri). These floats are displayed in the open during the morning time for all to see and admire. Other features of the Takayama Matsuri include:

- *Karakuri Performance* – these are mechanical dolls that can dance and move.

- *Mikoshi Procession* – A mikoshi procession takes place on both days of both the festivals, starting and ending in the respective shrines. The kami of the shrines come out only for the matsuri to bless the community of Takayama.
- *Evening Revelry* – The floats are taken on a procession through the streets of Takayama. The entire exercise can take anywhere between two and three hours.

Tenjin Maturi held at Tenmangu Shrine, Osaka

This annual two-day festival (July 24th and 25th) is dedicated to the kami of Sugawara Michizane who is enshrined in the Tenmangu Shrine. He was a celebrated poet and scholar of the Heian period. After his death, he became a kami and the god of art, learning, and calligraphy.

The Tenjin Matsuri is over 1000 years old, and yet the festive spirit today is replete with dance, music, and yatai (food stalls). The second day of the festival is the most important day when participants dressed in Heian costume take part in the procession which moves from the streets of Osaka to torch-lit boats that float along the Okawa River. There is a dazzling firework display at the end of the festival. The view of the flaming fireworks over the beautifully lit boats floating on the Okawa River is spectacular.

Awa Odori Matsuri held in Tokushima

This dance festival is easily the most popular and famous dance festivals in Japan happening during the Obon season (around Mid-August). Tokushima Prefecture was earlier known as Awa. Also referred to as the 'Fools' Dance,' this festival attracts dancers and spectators from all over the world.

The Awa Odori Matsuri is believed to have originated more than 400 years ago when a local leader (daimyo) in the Awa Province decided to celebrate the completion of the Tokushima Castle on a grand scale. Everyone got so drunk in that party that all got up and started swaying, singing, and playing musical instruments. Slowly, they created a simple melody for the party which ended up a dance party, and even today, that melody is played during the Awa Odori Festival.

Women dress in cotton robes (the yukata) and men wear happi, which is a shorter version of yukata. Designated spectator areas, called enbujo, are where the dances take place. In the evenings during the festival, the entire city center of Tokushima shuts down, and becomes one large dance stage where dancers and spectators join in the rather raucous revelry.

Matsuri, or Shrine Festivals, are performed primarily to appease and honor the kami of the shrine. The celebrations are all steeped in antiquity and age-old traditions that have been carried on for centuries. In fact, matsuri-goto is a term that translates to 'affairs of religious festivals,' and this term is commonly used to denote 'government.' This meaning aligns with the ancient belief that the business and task of the state is to conduct proper Shinto rites and ceremonies.

Chapter 7: Shinto in the Modern Era

Shinto has survived centuries of changes in Japan. Starting with its ancient origins in the prehistoric era, Shinto was almost lost and merged with Buddhism. However, it was repeatedly revived by followers and leaders of the Shinto faith with help and patronage from the Imperial Palace.

In 1867 during the Meiji Restoration, Shinto was formally separated from Buddhism and was made the state religion. At the end of WWII, Shinto was removed as the state religion in an attempt to squash Japanese aggression. However, Shinto continues to be the center of Japanese social and political life. Ancient Shinto rites and practices continue to thrive even in the technologically advanced modern Japanese society.

Importance of Shinto Rituals in Daily Life

Shinto rituals are mostly centered on life events such as birth, weddings, purification processes, and more. When a child is born, there is a seven-night celebration when the family takes the newborn to visit a Shinto shrine for the first time. A visit to a shrine done almost within a month of being born reflects the importance that the modern Japanese give to Shintoism and its rituals and rites.

Nearly all the local shrines are maintained and managed by the local community and the daily life of an average modern Japanese citizen is deeply involved with religion in general, and Shintoism, in particular. A common adage in Japan goes as follows: the Japanese marry as per Shinto faith, live their lives based on Confucian ethics, and are buried as per Buddhist rites.

So, religion is Japan is inextricably intertwined into the daily life with Shintoism joining hands with Confucianism and Buddhism. The three religions form part and parcel of every Japanese life with regard to the three most important aspects, birth, living, and death.

In modern Japan, Folk Shinto is believed to be most practical and useful to give meaning and value to the everyday existence. This primitive indigenous religion is replete with distinctive features from shamanism, magic, and divination with no rigid organization, or doctrines, but rather a simple custom of rites and rituals that are practiced by the people of the local communities.

Folk Shinto emphasizes rituals rather than esoteric metaphysical ideas. How, when, and where to conduct matsuri, how to appease and honor the kami and our ancestors, etc are all stressed. When following Folk Shinto beliefs and rituals, people expect immediate tangible results such as cure from an illness, prosperity in the family, getting a job, etc. The stress of rituals is on the power of the divine to grant you wishes that will make your life happy and prosperous.

Ancestor worship is another Shinto practice that is continued to this day. Whether it is in the form of visiting graves to make offerings or participating in the Obon festival in honor of ancestor spirits or conducting rituals in the kamidana, all reflect the importance that the modern Japanese give to ancestor worship. This attitude is also based on the Shinto faith which believes that ancestor spirits are like kami and watch over and protect their descendants, their household lineage, and family members, as long as the living conducts rituals and rites in their honor.

Daily activities of ancestor worship include offering of incense, food, and flowers to the ancestors at the kamidana. Yearly rituals are in the form of Obon festivals, New Year's first shrine visit, and the matsuri.

O-bon, typically in mid-August, is an important ancestor worship ritual for all families. During this time, traditional lanterns are hung outside the homes to guide the ancestors, Obon dances are performed, and food offerings are made at grave sites, houses, and shrines. At the end of the Obon festival, lanterns are set afloat on rivers, seas, and lakes to enable ancestor spirits to go back to their land. Many people return to their homeland from cities and towns to participate in the Obon festival and receive their ancestors' blessings.

Strangely though, nearly 80% of modern Japanese claim they do not belong to any one religion. Yet, they all visit shrines on New Year's Day, they visit and pay respects to graves of their ancestors, and they take off from work and visit the village they originally came from during the Obon festival; all of these are practices of the Shinto faith.

Amalgamation of Religions in Japan If you were to conduct an Internet search with keywords 'Japan religion,' the results are images of Shinto shrines with red torii, the quintessential Shinto symbol. Yet, religion in Japan goes beyond the archetypal rituals and structures that govern religion in other countries. The Japanese people practice Shinto rites and rituals, but they don't really engage with any religion. This attitude is quite contrary to the Western world. The concept of religion did not exist in Japan until the advent of the Western world into its land in the 19th century. During the Meiji period, Japan opened its doors to the Western world which brought the idea of religion as being a set of rules, regulations, and customs that are practiced and followed by the people who profess that particular religion. Religions, as per western concepts, are mutually exclusive. This strong and powerful idea that threatened to kill the existing culture of the country was counterbalanced by declaring Shinto as the state religion in 1867.

Otherwise, religion is taken casually in Japan as a matter of personal choice and preference which include additions from other religions and modifications of existing norms to suit the times and needs of the people. Finding Buddhist temples within Shinto shrines is common (not uncommon is a double negative). Most of the Japanese homes will have a Buddhist altar as well as Shinto kamidana.

Rituals are also interchanged. Funeral rituals are as per Buddhist practices whereas marriages and births are as per Shinto practices. Yet, no conflict or contradiction in the lives of the modern Japanese exists which could be due to the fact that this amalgamation of religions is an old concept in this ancient country.

However, despite the amalgamation, certain elements are considered purely Shinto-based, including aesthetic harmony with nature, ancestor worship, and purification rituals. Shinto has sacred texts based on which certain principles of living are derived. However, there are no set doctrines that govern the way of life in Shintoism unlike other religions such as the Bible for the Christians or the Koran for the followers of Islam.

Shintoism is considered less as a religion and more as a way of life by the modern Japanese. This attitude is an ancient as Shinto. In fact, Shinto has permeated the daily lives of the Japanese people that most are not even conscious of the fact that they are following age-old Shinto customs and rituals.

The shrine rebuilding process is an important feature of Shintoism still in practice, especially of the Ise Shrine, the grandest and the most revered Shinto Shrine in Japan. The regular rebuilding process has been taking place once in 20 years since 690 A.D., with only a small interruption. This rebuilding process is primarily to rejuvenate the power and influence of the kami of the shrine. The core intention of any Shinto ritual is to please and honor the kami.

Even the festivals or matsuri that are conducted are reminiscent of Shinto faith. Festivals are events when food offerings are made, music is played, with a lot of dancing, and Noh plays are performed. All these matsuri elements are based on the original purpose of making food offerings and participating in song and dance (even vulgar ones) to please the kami because kami resides in the highest achievements of art, food, and music.

Influence of Shintoism in Modern Japanese Politics and Society

While amalgamation of religions, acceptance of all forms of faith, etc are prominent features of Japanese society, a new, perhaps, disturbing trend is also setting in. The modern materialistic Japanese society is beginning to experience conflicts with its age-old religious beliefs. Very few countries in the world have the traditions, customs, and values from the past coexisting with modern ideas and concepts, which is a persisting contradiction fairly evident in today's Japanese society. The wide divide between the old and the new has its own set of repercussions on the people and society.

The Shinto faith spurns materialistic pleasures and individual growth as these are expected to be sacrificed for the welfare of the community and nation. However, modern perspectives are in stark contrast to this view. The consumer-driven society in Japan that has grown by leaps and bounds has made the country a leading industrial nation in East Asia. The technological and economic growth of Japan rivals the most advanced countries of the west.

The Japanese has access to an unprecedented supply of goods and materials making their lives not just comfortable but also very luxurious. The capital city, Tokyo, is a bustling metropolis rivaling the best of the best metropolitan cities of the world. In such a scenario, old-world Shinto-based social and religious messages seem to be in conflict with modern ideas.

These conflicts are becoming increasingly obvious as modern Japan shifts its base from group needs to individual needs and desires. Also, many Japanese are struggling to align Shinto faiths and beliefs with the perspectives of the outside world that they see and experience. Yes, there are many protests and sloganeering among the urban dwellers to want to return to the old traditional way of life. However, nothing concrete is happening in that regard as most would take the side of inevitability of change to counter the desire to revert to the old (and yes, less luxurious) way of life than what the modern society offers.

Surveys conducted on children show disturbing results, too. An international survey asked children this one question among others: "Do you feel worthless at times?" An overwhelming 84% of the kids answered 'yes.' This figure is double that of the US, China, and South Korea. The leaders of the country know, believe, and appreciate the fact that unless something is done to change this response, the country's future could be bleak.

Some of the remedies that a few politicians want to bring into student life are patriotic and moral lessons, respect for nationalism and the national symbols, and respect and dignity for the unique history and culture of Japan. These leaders are looking at changing textbooks that undermine nationalism. They are making efforts to reinstate the Emperor to a more prominent position. These changes are intended to undo some of the historical wrongs and reinstate the importance nationalistic pride along with keeping an eye on the positives that the future holds.

The Association of Shinto Shrines, a religious administrative organization, represents over 80,000 shrines spread all across the country and is an integral part of the Japanese government. Many of the top leaders of the country are part of this organization which has taken upon itself to revive the denigrating nationalistic and spiritual values of Japanese society. This association is openly antagonistic against policies that allow non-Japanese to buy strategic property such as lakes or forests. Many more political leaders are aligning themselves to the values and principles preached and advocated by the ancient Shinto religion including the divine lineage of the emperor.

In fact, shrines of people considered war criminals have been getting political sanctity in the recent past as top leaders visited these shrines. Those in favor of these changes argue that in today's perspective those warriors may look like war criminals. But at that time they only did what they believed was best for their country, and therefore, they need to be revered. Many people, including those among the influential and the elite, are keen on restoring the old glories of the Shinto faith. The turning point was World War II when the old Shinto faith was replaced by a more modern and democratic way of thinking. Today, the desire to go back to the old ways has its own set of challenges, including the changing roles of the household or 'ie', the unceasing urbanization and industrializations with the enormous benefits and conveniences they bring, and huge economic changes, which puts Japanese religious thoughts in direct conflict with modern life.

Yet, this conflict was not unexpected by the wise Japanese men of yore. As early as the 1600s, Japan adopted an isolation policy from the rest of the world in an attempt to maintain its national integrity. For over 200 years, Japan was completely isolated by curtailing all foreign trade. Then, in 1853, Matthew Perry came to Japan to deliver a letter requesting (or rather demanding) it to not only renew trading with the U.S. but also allow the American ships to fuel at the port of Nagasaki.

He came back the following year for the Emperor's response, and the might of the US naval ships that accompanied him did what it was supposed to do, compel Japan to open its doors for the U.S. In addition to fear, the Americans brought with them irresistible elements of convenience, luxury, and pleasure including a miniature locomotive which turned the Japanese tide in favor of industrialization. Being the amazing cultural borrowers they already are, the Japanese society and people quickly adapted to industrialization and leveraged its many benefits.

By 1900s, Japan became a powerful industrial nation in its own right. During the late 1900s, the Meiji restoration began which included the abolishment of the samurais, expanding its military, and fast modernization. They were unwilling partners with the West and entered the path to modernization under duress from the West. The Meiji period was one of immense changes in which Buddhism was more or less suppressed, and Shintoism was made the state religion. This period ended with WWII when Shintoism was abolished as the state religion, and Japan charged towards industrialization and modernization even faster.

While the Japanese people accepted their role to become a modern nation dutifully, most of them could see the contradictions between the philosophies of the modern age and those that were preached by their Buddhism-laced Shinto faith. This conflict continues to this day, and hopefully, the new emerging young generation will find the wherewithal to combine the best of both and take the country forward. Although there are conflicts in the modern Japanese society (which society in the world does not have conflicts?), there is little doubt that Shintoism and Japan are synonymous.

Conclusion

Everything in the world of Shintoism revolves around the kami which is the central core of this ancient religion that began as animism. Shinto slowly but gradually picked up ideas and thoughts from other religions, and has evolved into one undying faith that is unique to the country of Japan. It, therefore, makes sense to end this book with a small list of the most important kami (in this context, Shinto gods, goddesses, and spirits) in the Shinto religion, of which there are eight million kami.

Jizo – is the kami of childbirth and children. As per Shinto faith, children who die before their parents cannot cross the Sanzu River to reach the underworld are condemned to stacking little stones on its shores for eternity.

Jizo has the power to help such children cross the dreaded river. There are Jizo statues in multiple shrines across Japan mostly donated by parents who have lost their children. Leaving toys, bibs, and other baby things to appease this kami is common practice. Sometimes, stacks of stones are also left as offerings, perhaps, as a reminder to Jizo to help their children who are stacking stones on the shores of the Sanzu River.

Raijin and Fujin – Raijin is the kami of storms, lightning, and thunder in the Shinto religion. He is typically seen holding hammers and surrounded by drums. The kami of winds is Fujin, and he holds a bag of wind in his hand.

These two kami always come together, and they are a feared duo because of their ability to cause havoc and destruction through typhoons and storms. Even though they are fearsome, Raijin and Fujin also appear as guardian kami at the gates of shrines.

There is a myth used by Japanese parents who tell their children to cover their bellybuttons during typhoons and storms lest Raijin eat them up.

Inari – is the kami of almost everything that is important. She is a female kami, and goddess of tea, rice, fertility, sake, and material and worldly success. Foxes are her messengers because these animals are highly respected and revered in Shinto religion with shrines for foxes as well as statues of foxes in many of the shrines. The divine messengers of Inari love the delicious aburaage, and therefore, offerings are made to the shrines of foxes. Aburaage is tofu that is thinly sliced and deep-fried using an elaborate process. This process helps to harden the ever-so-soft tofu and make it tastier than before.

Ebisu – is the god of fisherman, dressed in formal court garments. He carries a fishing rod in his right hand and a huge red snapper in his left hand. He is a popular god among fishermen, sailors, farmers, and also people in the food industry. Ebisu's story is quite unique. He was born without bones, and even survival was painful for the child. When he was two years old, he was put into a boat and cast out to sea.

Ebisu managed to survive the rough seas grew bones. Many years later, he returned from the sea as a kami. Since then, he has been worshipped as the kami of fishermen and sailors. He is also one of the seven Japanese good luck gods and a protector of the health of the little children.

Ebisu is depicted as a round chubby person holding a fish and a fishing rod. Of course, today, his image is best known as the one on Yebisu beer cans; Japan's premium beer brand.

Taira no Masakado – Like Sugawara Michizane, Taira was a mortal who became a kami after his death. He challenged the Imperial Palace of Kyoto for it wrongdoing and fought against it and took over a large part of Japan. He was, however, defeated in 940 A.D. After his death, his head was brought to Tokyo and enshrined in the Kanda Shrine. The famous Kanda Matsuri is held in his honor. Before his revolt against the Imperial Regime in Kyoto, there were earthquakes, lunar eclipses, swarms of butterflies, and rainbows appearing all over Kyoto. Today, Taira is considered to be one of the most powerful kami, and he must constantly be appeased lest he brings bad luck and misfortune. The Shinto faith believes that kami are not only gods and spirits, but they are also the essence of being or existence. Everyone is empowered to exhibit their kami. They just need to find the strength and courage to see it and use it to do good things for the universe.

Bonus

As a way of saying thanks for your purchase, we're offering a special gift that's exclusive to my readers.

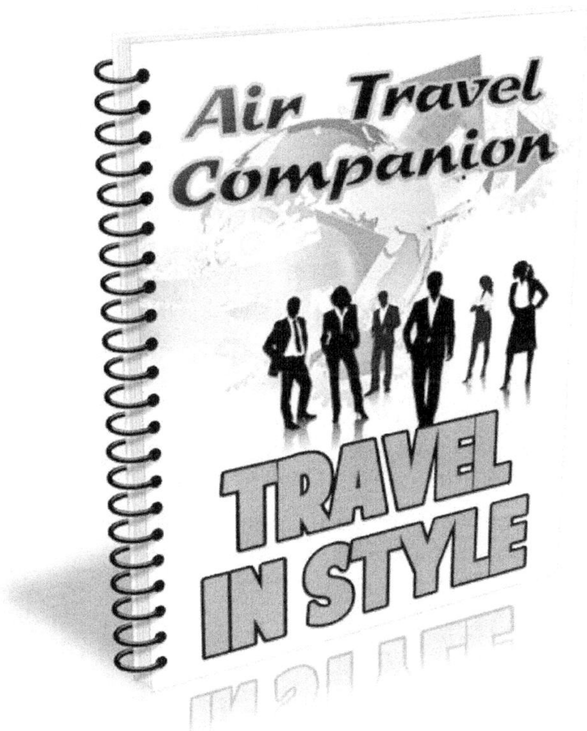

Visit this link below to claim your bonus.

http://dingopublishing.com/bonus/

MORE BOOKS FROM US

Visit our bookstore at: http://www.dingopublishing.com

Below is some of our favorite books:

RAMEN
NOODLES COOKBOOK
The Top 50 Delicious
Ramen Recipes To Cook At Home
LINDA NGUYEN

THE TOP 99 DELICIOUS RECIPES TO
FIGHT CANCER AND RESTORE YOUR HEALTH
ANTI-CANCER
Diet
Olivia Green

INTERMITTENT
FASTING
THE ULTIMATE GUIDE TO BURN FAT
AND BUILD LEAN BODY
JONATHAN SMITH

HIIT
BURN FAT AND BUILD LEAN BODY FASTER WITH
HIGH INTENSITY INTERVAL TRAINING
JOSHUA KING

Thanks again for purchasing this book.

We hope you enjoy it

Don't forget to claim your free bonus:

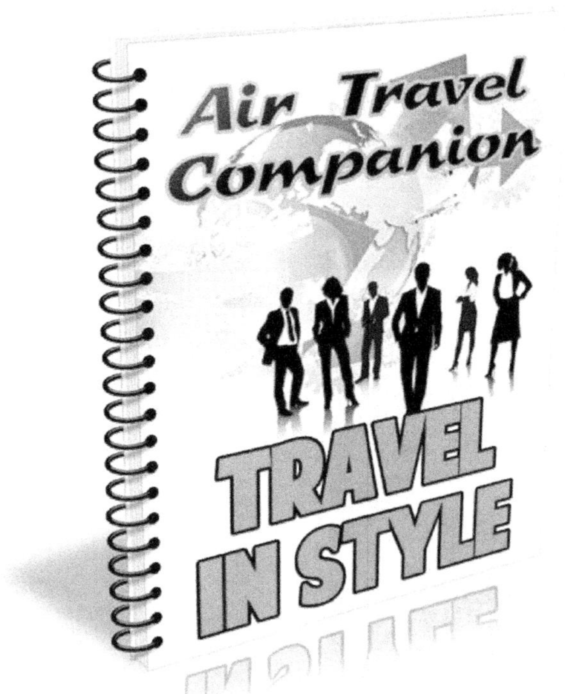

Visit this link below to claim your bonus:

http://dingopublishing.com/bonus/

Printed in Great Britain
by Amazon

41402938R00078